Valentino

66 And a work of beauty stands firm as a work of beauty, no matter what is blowing on the wind. **99**

Gerry Dryansky

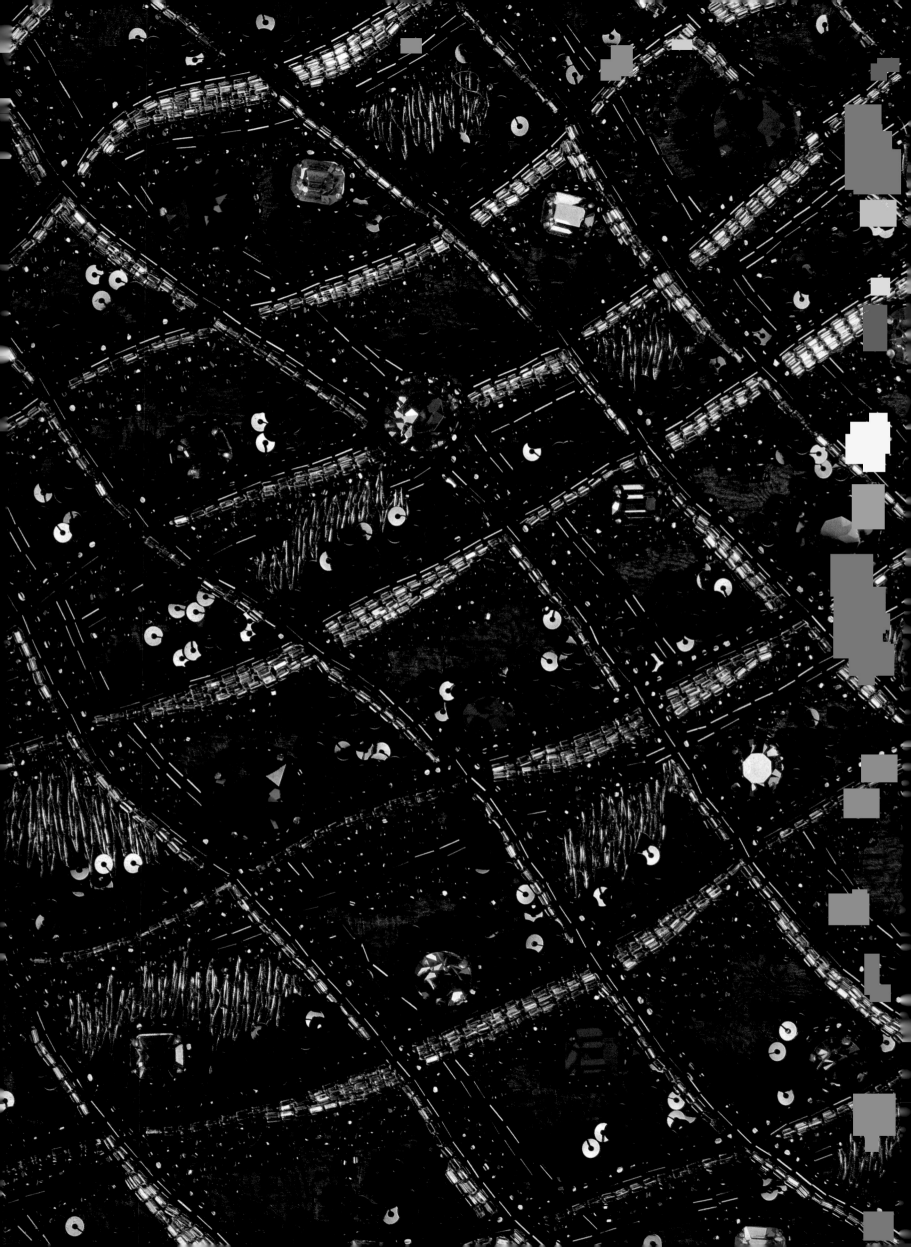

VALENTINO

THIRTY YEARS OF MAGIC

by
Marie-Paule Pellé

text by
Patrick Mauriès

With contributions by
François Baudot

Gerry Dryansky

Bonizza Giordani Aragno

Michael Gross

Art Director
Angelo Bucarelli

Abbeville Press • Publishers
New York • London • Paris

Haute Couture. Fall-Winter 1990-91.
Top covered with embroidery inspired by the late Italian Renaissance.
Photo Alfa Castaldi/Courtesy *Vogue* © 1990 Edizioni Condé Nast S.p.A.

ACKNOWLEDGMENTS

The publisher wishes to thank Valentino Garavani and Giancarlo Giammetti, who consented to the production of this book.

Special thanks to the photographers: Marella Agnelli, Mark Arbeit, David Bailey, Alexandre Bailhache, Dick Ballarian, Serge Barbeau, Giampaolo Barbieri, Cecil Beaton, François Leroy Beaulieu, Jonathan Becker, Leombruno Bodi, Sergio Caminata, Alfa Castaldi, Alex Chatelain, Walter Chin, Henry Clarke, Michel Comte, Attilio Concari, Bela Cseh, Gary Deane, Alberto Dell'Orto, Patrick Demarchelier, Bernard Descamps, Terence Donovan, Sante D'Orazio, Arthur Elgort, Fabrizio Ferri, Robert Frankenberg, Robert Freson, Danilo Frontini, Giovanni Gastel, Isidoro Genovese, Cristina Ghergo, Gianni Giansanti, Oberto Gili, Marco Glaviano, Jean-Pierre Goudeaut, Janos Grapow, Renato Grignaschi, Elsa Haerter, François Halard, J. Noël L'Harmeroult, Hiro, Marc Hispard, Peter Hönnemann, Horst P. Horst, Frank Horvat, Daniel Jouanneau, Art Kane, Eddy Kohli, Bob Krieger, Susan Lamér, François Lamy, Marco Lanza, Barry Lategan, David Lees, Peter Lindbergh, Stan Malinowsky, Stefano Massimo, Eamonn J. McCabe, Barry McKinley, Steven Meisel, Avi Meroz, Sheila Metzner, Sarah Moon, Walter Mori, Ugo Mulas, Nadir, Helmut Newton, Carlo Orsi, Norman Parkinson, Irving Penn, Denis Piel, Daniel Povda, Rico Puhlmann, Karen Radkaï, Vittoriano Rastelli, Jim Reiher, Regi Relang, Willy Rizzo, Matthew Rolston, Herbert Rowan, Galen Rowell, Franco Rubartelli, Satoshi Saikusa, Francesco Scavullo, Lothar Schmidt, David Seidner, Bill Silano, Lord Snowdon, Bob Stern, John Swannell, Mario Testino, Toni Thorimbert, Alberta Tiburzi, Oliviero Toscani, Deborah Turbeville, Tyen, Pietro Vaccari, Javier Vallhonrat, Fritz von der Schulenburg, Ellen von Unwerth, Chris von Wangenheim, Albert Watson, Alexandre Weinberger, Claus Wickrath, Susan Wood, Yokosuka.

Sincere thanks to the illustrators: Rodger Duncan, Mats Gustavson, Michael Meyring.

Thanks also to the models: Amalia, Amira, Daniela Azzone, Paloma Bailey, Benedetta Barzini, Stefania Belletti, Marisa Berenson, Bonnie Berman, Brinja, Pat Cleveland, Dalma, Diane de Witt, Aly Dunne, Vanessa Duve, Gail Elliot, Linda Evangelista, Lisa Garber, Daniela Ghione, Simonetta Gianfelice, Giselle, Jill Goodacre, Jerry Hall, Patty Hanson, Anjelica Huston, Lauren Hutton, Iman, Elaine Irwin, Jasmine, Sarah Kapp, Laura Killer, Kirat, Elena Kodoura, Lynne Koester, Betty Lago, Yasmin Le Bon, Dona Luna, Magali, Marpessa, Maddalena Mosca, Elsa Peretti, Mirella Petteni, Paulina Porizkova, Lisa Ruttledge, Marina Schiano, Sonia Schnetzer, Danka Schröder, Khoudia Seye, Tara Shannon, Brooke Shields, Diamante Spencer, Isa Stoppi, Alberta Tiburzi, Christy Turlington, Rosanne Vela, Veruschka, Eva Vorris, Leslie Winner.

Further thanks to: Peter Arnold Inc., *Amica*, Camera Press, Condé Nast Publications, Inc., Condé Nast Verlag GmbH, *Donna*, Edizioni Condé Nast S.p.A., *Elle*, *Frankfurter Allgemeine Magazin*, *Harper's Bazaar Italia*, *Harpers & Queen Magazine*, *House & Garden*, Les Publications Condé Nast S.A., *Moda*, *Moda In*, Mondadori Press, Grazia Neri, *L'Officiel*, Sotheby's, Studio Filomeno, Sygma, Verlag Hans Schöner, Visual Team, *WWD*.

In the Maison Valentino the help of Daniela Giardina, Barbara Vitti, Carlos Souza, Loredana Di Fusco, Grazia Martino, and Violante Valdettaro was invaluable.

Editorial Direction
Nadine Bortolotti

Production and Layout
Giorgio Gardel

Photo Editor
Paola Carabelli

Translation
Lucia Borro
Carol Lee Rathman

Editing
Ready - Made, Milano

Junior Art Director
Tommaso Concina

Design Assistant
Valerio Calcagnile

Some of the illustrations in this book had to be reproduced
from different publications as the originals were no longer available

Every effort has been made to trace the ownership of all copyrighted material
in the picture sections. In the event of any question arising about the use of any
material, the authors and publisher, while expressing regret for any inadvertent
error, will be happy to acknowledge all respective rights.

© 1990 Leonardo Editore srl, Milano
I edition January 1990

Library of Congress Cataloging-in-Publication Data

Pellé, Marie-Paule.
Valentino: thirty years of magic / by Marie-Paule Pellé; text by Patrick Mauriès;
with contributions by François Baudot ... [et al.]. - 1st ed.
p. cm. ISBN 1—55859—237—7
1. Valentino. 2. Costume design—Italy. 3. Costume designers-Italy—
Biography. I. Mauriès, Patrick, 1952 - . II. Title.
TT507.P37 1990
746.9'.2'.092—dc 20
[B]
91-10337 CIP

Cover
Drawing Rodger Duncan.

Pages 4-5
Haute Couture. Fall-Winter 1984-85.
Detail of an embroidered tunic.
Photo Janos Grapow/Archivio Valentino.

Page 6
Sketch by Valentino.
Pencil and watercolor on cardboard, $10^{1}/_{2} \times 14^{1}/_{2}$ in.
One of the models Valentino did during his apprenticeship
at the Dessès atelier in Paris in the Fifties.
Rome, Archivio Accademia Valentino.

Page 11
Haute Couture. Fall-Winter 1965-66.
Left, white evening dress.
Photo Pietro Vaccari/Archivio Valentino.

W omen wearing Valentino do not toil in factories. They do not consider themselves commonplace. They do consider themselves in Cap d'Antibes, Claridge's, and Le Cirque.

Women wearing Valentino can be found lounging poolside in Capri. Skiing in Gstaad. Running board meetings in Manhattan. They can be anywhere, but they aren't everywhere. Valentino's women make a dinner meaningful and magnificent; they do not make dinner. I see them strutting down a long Paris runway — Jackie O., Jayne Wrightsman, Babe Paley, Gloria Guinness, Marella Agnelli — and striding forward in a line radiating power tempered by grace. Probably they are striding toward lunch in the garden at the Ritz, or in some *hôtel particulier* on the rue de Grenelle.

Look at them. You can't help it. Their necks are all long and erect, their shoulders straight, their stance kinetic, their legs lean and ready — always a step ahead.

Women wearing Valentino. They may like lace and fantasy but these are no Little Bo Peeps. Neither are they thoroughbreds, whippets or gazelles, though they have the legs for it. They are not cute. They are not coy. They are neither the victims nor the perpetrators of crimes of fashion.

They are not about Desire either. Rather, they are about certain highly cultivated desires. They are romantic. They are not easy.

Women wearing Valentino. For there are no such things as Valentino girls. There is nothing unformed about them. Not even Brooke Shields, who was still like a virgin when she appeared in a Valentino on the cover of *Time* magazine illustrating ''The Eighties Look.'' Some virgin. Even though Valentino's work harkens back to times past, it is rooted, strong as an ancient tree, in the contemporary idea and exercise of womanly power.

Even in dark glasses the eyes of Valentino's woman flash with knowledge. Even in a little nothing black dress, she is something. Really something.

''A woman must cause heads to turn when she enters a room,'' Valentino has said. ''A woman does not want to disappear.''

Valentino's woman sets heads spinning.

That's because women wearing Valentino have power that crosses national, political, professional, and social lines. His clique encompasses the wives and mistresses of Milanese industrialists, Roman countesses, and an Iranian empress, Italian and American first ladies, Niarchoses, Agnellis, Rothschilds, Fords, Lollobrigida, and Veruschka. And when these women cross lines of their own, quite often they wear Valentino.

Take Jacqueline Bouvier Kennedy on the day she married Aristotle Onassis. She was telling the world — and herself — something that day. And she chose a Valentino — a beige lace top and flyaway skirt. Couture, of course. Goodbye first lady. Hello Jackie O. What a knockout.

Women wearing Valentino are all different. Their line veers like a signature V from right bank to left bank, east coast to west, Farah Diba to Farrah Fawcett.

And yet, women wearing Valentino have more than a logo in common. Valentino women don't borrow their personality from clothes. Audrey Hepburn doesn't get her grace from a gown. Liz Taylor is never lost in her jewels and embroidery. Power like that wielded by Nancy Reagan or Georgette Mossbacher cannot be merely a matter of pale flesh and paper taffeta. Like them or not, these ''ladies'' are contenders.

Glamorous and elegant, softly tailored and a little conservative, but not unaware of the lures and lies of decadence, Valentino's women populate all the best places, knowing that they have what it takes to pass unmolested through even the worst of times.

Not that they see many bad times. Women wearing Valentino are simply a cut above.

Michael Gross

Page 12
Rome, 1972.
Valentino with his public
at the close of a show.
Photo Courtesy *Vogue* © 1972
Edizioni Condé Nast S.p.A.

Page 15
Haute Couture. Spring-Summer 1963.
Drawing Michael Meyring.

VOGUE
Paris

VALENTINO
Spring '63

Jacket,
zebra printed
calfskin —
jet-embroidered
passementerie

Skirt,
white silk

Worn by
Simone d'Aillencourt

he myth of the artist exists: forty years ago two Central European intellectuals conducted a scholarly study and wrote the definitive results in a few pages. The myth of the *couturier* also exists; but it has yet to be written, being a mere corollary of the former.

Valentino cannot be overlooked in this respect; indeed, he offers a shining example of it. As a child he paid no attention to activities supposedly suited "to his age"; he was not the least bit interested in fun and games, the small rivalries, the great inseparable friendships, the scoldings, and the ballgames; he was already obsessed with the paper sewing patterns that his aunt's notions business was so rich in; he was trying, and with some success, to sketch out figures and styles — auspicious foreshadowings of a pure dreamworld made up of quintessential forms, lightness, luxury.

This all happened in Voghera, a small town of Lombardy that would later claim Valentino, as they would have said in classical times, as its ornament. No foreigner can estimate what an Italian's "homeland" represents to him, adopted or by right of birth, roots that he fiercely defends and that define his very being once and for all. I once overheard a young girl in a restaurant shrug off a flaw in her companion's personality as due to his Brescian heritage. Every city, town, region, and neighborhood has its own creative principles that determine physiognomy and substance, culinary and aesthetic tastes, accents and erotic nuances — and especially world outlooks.

But this is the point: Valentino is one of those rare, aberrant Italians for whom geographical sentiments seem to have next to no importance. In Voghera he was born in 1932; there he lived out an apparently happy adolescence; and from Voghera he departed in 1950 to follow the path of his desire or his obsessions, not to return until many years later on the occasion of his deification, the above-mentioned recognition (you may forget your origins, but they never forget you).

Let us return to our discussion of the myth of the *couturier*. Ever since he can remember he dreamed of but one thing, one world; some years later (we are skipping way ahead) he found himself at the center of this world, as real as he had desired. This lightning course, this extraordinary blossoming, was ensured by just a few intermediaries, a handful of wild cards: a mother, Paris, one or more muses, a friend and partner.

Let us now trace the succession of events that helped to create the legend: episodes endlessly repeated, similar to what everybody has experienced in the immediate family circle, anecdotes rehashed over and over at ritual get-togethers until one cannot take it any more; or blown up with evident relish beyond all recognition by the press when it is a matter of "out of the ordinary" figures. Nevertheless, these scenes and fragments of stories manage to conserve, even after all the repetition, their exemplary and revelatory value.

So, there is a child who has eyes only for the materials and the textures that surround us, the shapes behind which we hide ourselves, and which we need. He demanded from his parents made-to-measure clothing in the finest wools and cashmeres, with *that* collar and *that* cut; he could not bear slovenliness, or lack of respect for one's person. At a young age, he chose only to see and to take interest in the "beautiful and the good," as the ancient Greeks would say; he could conceive only of a reality mastered, distilled, subjected to the law of aesthetics. Once he had to make an appearance at a little party given in honor of his cousin, though he was ill. He asked someone to help him over to admire his cousin's party attire, and the emotion aroused in him by the rustling fabric was so strong that to this day he remembers the rose-colored tulle dress that the fortunate young girl wore on that day; as he was to remember his wonder at the rustling of a black crepe de chine skirt with green polka dots made for his mother by the Costa sisters, renowned *couturières* of Voghera; or the soft-

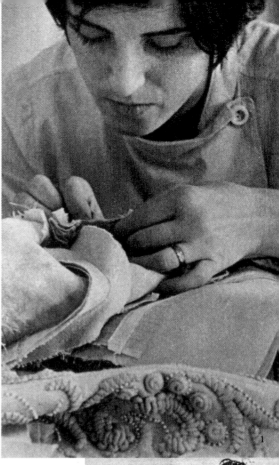

1 Rome. Laboratory: handcrafted workmanship of an Haute Couture dress. Photo Robert Freson/Archivio Valentino.
2 Haute Couture. Spring-Summer 1959. Valentino presents a print dress with crinoline skirt. Photo Archivio Valentino.
3 Rome, 1959. Valentino in his atelier at the work table. Photo Lord Snowdon/Archivio Valentino.

ness of a coat in *grain de poudre* trimmed with a fox-fur collar.

Nothing but passions, delectable passions; or, if you like, the signs of destiny. May it suffice to desire, said Nietzsche, to achieve one's happiness. And while Valentino's trajectory to success bears out this formula, it also goes to show that he always knew what he wanted, and that he unerringly followed the road that opened out before him, taking advantage of all the imponderables, the strokes of luck, predestinations, and complex legacies.

"An almost infantile belief," he says himself, "in the possibility of getting out of life what I want." To believe that all is allowed or possible has been the guiding light in his life, alongside a strange form of self-knowledge. In our everyday culture we are surrounded by references to astrology, and the fact of belonging to one of the signs (in this case, Taurus) is not always met with indifference; when it is not seen as an archaic holdover of superstitious beliefs, it seems to charge the person in question with an inrush of energies.

Another source, another presence, another inspiration behind Valentino's utter self-assurance, a figure of enormous psychological importance is the maternal figure. It is fascinating to think that behind the most resonant creations of today's fashion world — the ones that have enjoyed the greatest popular success — behind the revolution in our everyday appearance, stand a handful of elegant provincial ladies of mid-century, who were more decisive in the vicissitudes of fashion than the great buyers or other legendary figures in the history of elegance.

Look at how Saint Laurent, Lacroix, and Valentino evoke a mother's leaving for the ball, a trail of perfume, a hat (when it

1 1959. Valentino at a New York reception. Photo Archivio Valentino.
2 Haute Couture. Spring-Summer 1967. Valentino and his models.
Presentation of the collection at the Martha Award ceremony
in New York. Photo Archivio Valentino.
3 Haute Couture. Fall-Winter 1959-60. Ball gown with ivory-colored
satin cape. Photo Archivio Valentino.

was still *de rigueur*) with its halo of chiffon, a necklace, a cocktail dress carefully chosen for a meeting with her lady friends. These traces leave burning impressions on one's childhood and long after their disappearance leave a mark, like a retinal after-image upon our memory. Although fashion is seemingly the art most rooted in the present, it is in fact paradoxically supported by distant reminiscences imbued with happy nostalgia; it is the inevitable form of homage that a period pays to its yesterday.

Not that these involve solemn commemorations, nor do they refer to great moments or the most important events of a given period; rather they focus on a multitude of accents that make up the ordinary, and whose destiny is to disappear with their day. Traces of them remain in that slight moment of hesitation, suspended for just one last instant in such details as the design of a pocket, the cut of a sandal, the color of a taffeta, the pattern of a print.

At the age of fifteen, the young Valentino Garavani realized once and for all that it would be a mistake to continue in the field of geometrical sketches and drawings; his real interest lay in the freehand variations of fashion design. He calmly and frankly opened his heart to his parents and stated his intention to quit high school without taking his final examinations in order to take the plunge into the world of high fashion. There was the predictable moment of shock and alarm, which could only give way to resignation, given the young man's no less predictable determination. So, armed with his parents' blessing and his innately methodical approach to things, he spent a few months in Milan to study French and to take courses in fashion design at a school in via Santa Marta. It was a period of apprenticeship, a period of transition before setting his foot inside that magic ring — the place for which Valentino will never cease to feel an unremitting sense of awe: Paris, capital of clothing and of *savoir-faire*, of hostesses and balls, of the spirit of a time.

Valentino arrived in Paris in 1950. Three years earlier, a name had become a household word overnight. Dior took his place at the helm of fashion, launching a style that was to represent an epoch. It was a return to petticoat, to the eighteenth century revisited by Napoléon III, to Louis XVI style; it was the time when Arturo Lopez recreated a miniature Versailles in downtown Neuilly, Charles de Beistegui took possession of the Palazzo Labia in Venice, and Emilio Terry set his imagination to work on the ''Louis XVII'' style.

No less than twenty-five or twenty-six yards of taffeta were needed to obtain the volume of such suggestively named lines as *Corolle, Cyclone, Tulipe, Oblique, Sinueuse, Verticale*, not to mention the fifty yards of black plait that edged the neck- and hemlines of a 1947 model. Shameless expenditures, exaggerated shapes, and voluminous materials became all the rage in a society that had just emerged from the privations of the war. The contrast was striking: the daily economy was laboriously recovering while inordinate fortunes were being spectacularly squandered in a wild contest to achieve absolute luxury.

It was getting difficult, reported a society journal of the time, to keep track of "*les nuits de*" this and the "*les quinzaines de*" that. The two hundred fiftieth anniversary of the Place Vendôme was celebrated, the fiftieth of the Métro, the one hundred fiftieth of the Conseil d'Etat. Ladies arrived at the balls on camelback or carried in litters, dressed up as firebirds, Cleopatras, angels of Versailles, Lancret's Harlequins.

This was also the golden age of the sculptural and slender muses: Mitza Bricard and runway model Renée for Dior, Liza Fonsagrives for Irving Penn, Dovima for Avedon, Patricia Lopez Willshaw, Maxime de la Falaise, Audrey Hepburn; all crea-

Spring-Summer 1959.
Drawing by Valentino: Ibis line.

tures with long, swanlike necks underlined with pearls, accentuated by décolleté, with slim waists and hips emphasized by peplums; gloved, hatted, *soignées*, as the designer's pet word so aptly describes them.

Armed with a grant from the Chambre Syndicale de la Haute Couture Parisienne, Valentino landed in Jean Dessès's atelier where he stayed for five years, "like at university," before moving on to spend two years with Guy Laroche (of Dessès little else remains today but a perfume in a fine white felt-lined box, evocatively named "Bal à Versailles," the last trace of the sumptuous mid-twentieth-century dream). But the sparkle of this period seems to stem from a burning fascination with the art of living. He was discovering this in the salon of Jacqueline de Ribes, a graphic creature with high cheekbones, almond-shaped eyes, a remarkably fine nose, and tapered hands more suited to caressing things than to taking hold of them.

Unconsciously, she offered herself to a gaze dazzled by so much natural "civility." Valentino was fascinated by her three or four changes of *toilette* per day, by her way of serving tea, moving, selecting her attire, seating her guests, decorating a table, by her tone of voice, her love of accessories, the confidence of her gestures, a way of crossing her legs, a trail of perfume.

"*La donna immaginaria*," said a baroque Italian aesthete of the seventeenth century. The woman who does not exist, who has never been nor shall be, said Saint-Evremond; such is the dazzling specter that took root in Valentino's imagination and the styles he produced — in the form of so many flashes, flickers of memory, blazes of inspiration. This ideal woman oriented all of his later production, his concept of dress, without restricting him to a historical frame of reference or dating him.

It was an essence that was embodied in the rustling of taffeta; in the contour of a neckline; in a fabric that was never quite silky, abundant, rich, or sculptural enough for him; and in a boundless sensual pleasure in spending and in the imponderable.

After seven years of apprenticeship of unusual happiness, Valentino returned to Italy to open an atelier on via Condotti in Rome, near such stars — by then fading from the scene — as Schubert and the Fontana sisters. Boutiques that preserved a bit of the discretion, the intimate side of the family *couturier*, while still belonging by full rights to the exigent and extravagant world of the Haute Couture. This was also the peak season of such greats as Lancetti, Fabiani, Antonelli, Emilio Pucci, and a singular and rigorous architect named Roberto Capucci. The legendary designer took his first faltering steps; his parents offered him several million lire with which he financed his first *maison de couture*. And at this time Valentino was dealt the final winning card in his game, his alter ego: the man who filled, as the need arose, the posts of administrator and financier, a behind-the-scenes figure who made the dream possible.

July 30, 1960: sitting at an outdoor café on one of those seductively sweet Roman evenings, a young student of architecture watches the approach of a lively group led by a young man, a rising star of the Italian fashion scene who had already attracted notice for some remarkable accomplishments. Though we have no eyewitness reports, we are perfectly familiar with the scene, the toy shop and *parrucchiere* Millefiori to one side and the tobacconist on the other. The Café de Paris, bordered with flower pots, is saturated by a piercing light that dances in a glittering display over the chrome trim of cars, the lenses of dark glasses, coffee cups, and novelty brooches that the bescarved *mondaines* of the time were so fond of.

On via Veneto, then, of which we have a minutely detailed copy made in August of the previous year in Studio 5 of Cinecittà, as close in detail as it could be even if the original was sinuously sloping while the copy was quite flat and straight. Valentino and Giancarlo Giammetti met in the heart of a Rome that was in its full glory, in the height of its season of elegance. They crossed paths again in Capri, and when one of the young fashion designer's financiers wished to retire, causing not a few problems, the twenty-one-year-old architecture student stepped in to resolve the crisis.

Even before one piece was sold, the first Roman collection became the talk of the town, affronting the nonchalant provincialism of the capital when Valentino had, *alla grande*, enticed away one of Dior's top models to put on the runway in Rome. But the true fashion center was in Florence, the meeting ground for international buyers. After a hard-fought struggle Valentino won the right to show there, almost surreptitiously, at the end of the day when the buyers and journalists are saturated. But by word of mouth — the noble and profitable version of gossip, the true life-breath of the fashion world which hungrily gobbles up news about new names, fresh reputations, potential upstarts — the unknown designer's name reached the ears of some influential people. The first act of the golden legend of Valentino took place. He made his mark with one hundred pieces selling immediately. What has blossomed today into ten seasonal collections was just then beginning to germinate.

Nevertheless, gossip amounts to nothing without the aid of its high priestesses. And whether it was a question of luck or necessity, Valentino benefited from the kindness of an extraordinary constellation of darlings and other society ladies. Leafing through the earliest of the three hundred volumes of archives housed in piazza Mignanelli reveals his legions of diaphanous ladies of Rome. These aristocrats never stepped out of their homes if they were not dressed in Valentino's latest tailleur or evening gown. Indeed they were as good as models, slightly phantasmic as they put themselves on display: the Princesses Luciana Pignatelli, Orsetta Caracciolo Torlonia, Allegra Caracciolo di Castagneto, Peggy d'Arenberg, Ira Fürstenberg. But this dazzling array of elegance risks overshadowing other even more decisive figures, such as Consuelo Crespi, at the time the

pulse of the Roman ican edition of the mainsprings of success. He was the most flam- elegance, Diana platonic ideal of she was an un- with a profile like Manchurian em- poised to swoop *coup d'éclat* or the ("There must be absurdity or snob- the reigning ion kingdom, care- her eccentric distilling her meta- lous in a language Always on the herself on her in- was one of the Valentino's tal-

office of the Amer- *Vogue*, and one of Valentino's earliest also linked with boyant artist of Vreeland. As the the fashion editor, likely candidate, a gargoyle's or a press's, ever down on the next wildest innovation no limits to either bery."). She was queen of the fash- fully cultivating personality and physics of the frivo- rich with nuance. alert and priding tuition, Vreeland first to recognize ent, and she gave

Haute Couture. Spring-Summer 1989.
Valentino with Aly Dunne in a black silk evening dress.
Rome, Palazzo Mignanelli.
Photo Barry McKinley/Archivio Valentino.

him her support with a rare constancy. This was doubtless one of the fashion designer's main channels to success. From the very beginning he shot to international imnportance, endowed by a circle of prestigious clients, Americans as well as Europeans. "Valentino Steals Spotlight" ran a July 1965 headline in the *New York Times*, and three months later *Marie-Claire* dedicated several pages to "the crazy style of Virna Lisi" and "the new Italian *couturier* with the storybook name of Valentino" who was constantly "outdoing himself in extravagance."

The customers, ladies who represent a strange hybrid between the fairytale world and that of commerce, a royal universe and one of spectacle, pure innate grace and the expert make-over, the "black continent" as Freud described womanhood, at once far and near, familiar and unknown. It is a curious relationship that binds the fashion designer and his customer, comparable to that which we might have with an antiques dealer or to the tie between a patron and an artist. There is no doubt that it is an economic relationship, but one that also involves trust and consent and occasional rejection, going beyond the game of giving and receiving; they become accomplices in a form of partnership or sharing. Remarkably, from the very start — and thanks to the channels we mentioned above — Valentino's clientele extended beyond the select circles of Roman society to the other side of the Atlantic. Part of Valentino's fascination owes to the supereminence of his clientele, which includes countless first ladies, actresses, and prominent personalities, involves the whole spectrum of femininity, from the young girl to the mature woman, from the full complete form of a Sophia Loren to the budding one of a Brooke Shields. Valentino's styles also show an intriguing ability to set the pace of the times. There

Haute Couture. Spring-Summer 1989.
Giancarlo Giammetti in his studio with Aly Dunne.
Rome, Palazzo Mignanelli.
Photo Barry McKinley/Archivio Valentino.

is the famous winter coat in hazel-colored cashmere bordered in sable that Farah Diba wrapped herself in as she left for her exile. There is the little pleated skirt and lace bodice conceived for the Onassis wedding — a now legendary event — for which Valentino received no less than thirty-eight requests for copies, not necessarily coming from families of colossal wealth, but a good part of them from Italy. The canonic list of personalities in the Valentino pantheon includes Jackie Onassis and Princess Margaret, Jane Fonda and Brooke Shields, Marella Agnelli and Joan Collins, Sophia Loren and the queen of Jordan.

No doubt friendship networks and a genius for public relations contributed greatly to bringing together such a set of worldly female icons; but the phenomenon is much simpler and more natural to explain. It arises from the nature of fashion design itself as Valentino knows it, his almost childlike sensual delight in sumptuous and delicate fabrics, ornate bits of embroidery, rich, deep colors, all those elements that can exalt an ideal and truly magical femininity, which in his mind can never be too extravagant, caressing, or sophisticated. It is a form of theater that is never better interpreted than by the incredible, exaggerated, filtered, altered humanity that is conferred by celebrity.

In this respect, Valentino has never changed his course. Resuming our chronological account, a photo of Veruschka that dates from about the time when the firm was established describes this personality perfectly. It is an icon of femininity in full bloom and almost cunning, a perfect enchantress Alcina, a baroque fairy witch with a broad forehead and light-colored eyes, hieratic and sensual, made-up and bejeweled, with an incredible mane of hair, the symbol of that alluring and secret otherness whose flamboyance itself is a weapon. Rarely has a model so effectively used a kind of bestiality. Veruschka's beauty arises from abnormal proportions, too-large lips and eyes, a too-fine nose, an excess of hair, feline proportions, the nimbleness of her limbs, the slenderness of waist, a bend of the wrist, a certain stride, a way of curling back on herself. The effect is a slight inebriation, a subtle unsettling, an invisible entropy of what is human. And every square inch of this extraordinary machine exuded an extreme civility that could not help but give perfect substance to Valentino's obsession with the *soigné*. ("*Soigné* is the word," he said to an English journalist, "such a pity you have no English translation.")

Valentino knows intuitively that despite the illusion that accompanies our daily lives, the human body is above all made up of bits and pieces, of mismatched elements, a problem that only a master craftsman can solve by going deeper into the illusion, searching for a vision of the whole, for a harmony that is by nature ephemeral (a penchant that finds expression in the garment industry terms total look or *coordonnées*). And everybody who has ever worked with him will bear witness to the fashion designer's care to ensure that not a model steps out onto the runway who is not perfectly coiffed, made up, perfumed, fit out with shoes, gloves, and jewelry. Extreme vigilance and methodical construction combine to create the most natural air, the most fluid movements.

Starting in 1965, Valentino's career took on the non-stop rhythm of the different seasonal "themes" in an endless succession of "lines" and "trends." The year 1968 saw the launch of the "Collection blanche" in which for the first time the *couturier's* production bore what was to become a personal hallmark: the use of white, which appears like a leitmotif through all of his years of activity, has resurfaced in new form in the recent Hoffmann-inspired collections with their contrasting black filigree. The following years showed uncertainty about hemlines. "The miniskirt is dead once and for all. I believe that the midi is the only chance for a return to elegance," he said in an interview of 1970. Certainly, the period was marked by dramatic contrasts and reversals of tendency. The conflict hinged on a simple choice between the fresh new design of the "mini," risqué and not for everybody, and its utter opposite, a historical reference that returned women to the long-forgotten shapes of the first decades of the century. It was an unexpected swing full of exotic overtones.

The year 1967 marked the release of a film that heralded this sharp return to the past and the presentation of a nostalgic and romantic collection: *Bonnie and Clyde*, directed by Arthur Penn. Though many years have passed, we must not overlook the fact that it ushered in an era focusing on the curious events of the 1930s and initiating a vogue that would not pass until twenty years later — after an incredible reevaluation of the style and its subjects. At the time, the English proposed dubbing this style "Longuette," but the few attempts to make it stick with the press fell through; instead Barbara Hulaniki's Biba stores headed up the commercial success of this new fashion, offering it in a hybrid form to the general public in a wide variety of inexpensive articles and clothing. Black and gold were the colors that dominated the fashion world. In less than five months the modernism and wild prints of the miniskirt era gave way to a wave of nostalgia in classical hues tending toward dark colors and straight lines. ("There is a lot of op," wrote Irene Brin in the *Giornale d'Italia* of July 20, 1965, "in the Valentino collection … checkered, lozenged and striped patterns in black and white used in a variety of ways on short coats or suits and white blouses.")

Again it was demonstrated that, like painting in classical times or opera in the nineteenth century, film is the most important and most influential art of this century. In 1969 Luchino Visconti's *The Damned* was released, and Valentino does not deny his fascination with the film's main character, his world, and his imagination, nor that they were a source of inspiration for several collections of the time. This aristocrat with finely chiseled features, a great narcissistic and brusque

Haute Couture. Fall-Winter
1967-68.
Valentino on the runway of his
Rome atelier with three models
wearing evening gowns: the first
in a brocade print inspired by
Persian carpet motifs; the second
in crepe with embroidered
garlands was later worn by
Jacqueline Onassis in Cambodia.
Archivio Valentino.

lord aware of his heritage and sure of his tastes and of his yearnings after the past, showed Valentino not so much a unique aesthetic or a vague pleasure in "decadence" or a deleterious fascination for virulent beauty, but rather the importance of lifestyle, of the art of living. Because, if Visconti championed a value in his life and his work, it was certainly that of aesthetics applied to the most insignificant details of our lives, to the film set as well as to a place setting for a meal, interior decoration, and conversation. The 1969-70 and 1976-77 collections are steeped in nostalgia.

In 1972 Valentino presented an Edwardian line exploiting once again this aristocratic nostalgia in its dying burst of glory. There is a long flounced skirt in a large check pattern accompanied by a transparent *faux plis* blouse with leg-of-mutton sleeves and very high collar edged with lace ruches — a nostalgic and refined style destined to an Arcadia of conventions, a rustling reverie. In retrospect it can be seen how such a play of proportions and volumes, the way of concealing the figure behind the fullness of the fabric, the rejection of structure behind this style that hovers somewhere between the peasant and the gypsy, is now outdated in most of Europe, England excepted, additional proof that the "English scene" is the only one today (I am talking about what one sees in the streets) where skirts that drop to below the knees are still familiar and commonplace. This indicates a typical Victorianism as well as a deluxe bohemian style, an obstinate casualness, mildly transgressive, as Virginia Woolf or Vanessa Bell practiced it: headscarf and leather sandals.

Valentino was not inclined toward the very long, the very loose-fitting, the woolen and calico fabrics typical of the country look. Nevertheless, from his synthetic "Velázquez Gypsy Look" of 1969 to the Tyrolian accents of 1977 to certain articles from more recent collections, he has remained faithful throughout his long career to folk motifs. Depending on the occasion, he borrows from the Arabic, Slavic, Indian, and Chinese traditions.

This could represent one of the poles of recurrent opposites in his work: that of the light, veiled, transparent fabrics versus the heavily embroidered vests, bodices, and tunics with inlay work, beads, or encrusted with multicolored threads and rhinestones that offset the suppleness of the rest, as if the designer found a point of contact with the ancient masters.

Another "ethnic" resonance emerges when visiting the meticulously kept clothing collection housed on one floor of the Palazzo Mignanelli. Very early on, Valentino showed a predilection (particularly in evening gowns) for the quilted fabrics that one often finds in the mountain regions. He also often returns to the muted tones of the loden fabrics that are typical of the southern Alps. In 1977 he

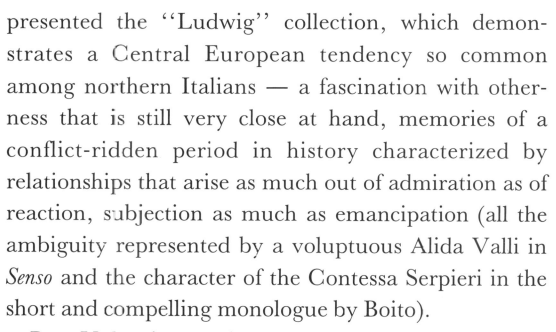

presented the "Ludwig" collection, which demonstrates a Central European tendency so common among northern Italians — a fascination with otherness that is still very close at hand, memories of a conflict-ridden period in history characterized by relationships that arise as much out of admiration as of reaction, subjection as much as emancipation (all the ambiguity represented by a voluptuous Alida Valli in *Senso* and the character of the Contessa Serpieri in the short and compelling monologue by Boito).

But Valentino arrived at this rich and diverse Central Europe through yet another device, one that makes up another constant feature of his output. In 1973 he presented a collection whose printed fabrics (for the most part crepe georgette) took their inspiration from Gustav Klimt and a series of sumptuous dresses whose exuberant patterns and vibrant colors

1 Valentino in his atelier with Virna Lisi wearing a dress that made history from the Spring-Summer 1965 collection. Photo Angelo Frontoni. 2 Gustav Klimt, detail of the dining room in the Stoclet palace. Brussels, 1905-11. 3 Haute Couture. Fall-Winter 1989-90. Shoe with embroidered motif inspired by the Jugendstil. 4 Valentino in his atelier with styles from the Fall-Winter 1967-68 collection. Photo Walter Mori/*Epoca* © Mondadori Press.

Page 33
Haute Couture. Fall-Winter 1962-63. Yellow lace dress on the film set for Fellini's *8½.*
Photo Archivio Valentino.

may well have been in homage to Léon Baskt. Fifteen years later Hoffmann was the inspiration behind the rigorous two-toned color scheme in a line that reproposed the stylized patterns of Wiener Werkstätte's friezes and ogives. This decoration was similar to that of the halls of the Accademia that Valentino opened in 1989 next door to the Palazzo Mignanelli. The Viennese never declared — as Adolf Loos did — that decoration was a crime; rather they sought a return to both the logic and the lexicon of traditional ornament through novel applications in cabinetry, architecture, and the design of ordinary objects. Valentino shows a similar predilection when he appliqués motifs abstracted from the work of Hoffmann or others onto an article of clothing. He enjoys treating fashion as another of the decorative arts. The dress with dots and sinuous lines that he designed in 1989 is simultaneously a citation, an homage, and a creation in its own right subject to a new order, a new logic, and thus achieving utterly new associations.

Let us return to the hushed floor of the Palazzo Mignanelli, with its sound-muting wall-to-wall carpeting, mirrored walls, and metal stands where the articles of clothing are carefully conserved. Labeled, described, classified, covered, cleaned, restored, they are like a very alive memento, an arresting panorama of thirty years of activity. Giancarlo Giammetti explains with a smile how this museum was put together. Nobody even remotely suspected twenty years ago the extraordinary cultural dignity that would invest these remains of a daily effort, these fragile combinations of fabrics, whose fate would have been to disappear with their time, to end up forgotten in the back of some closet. Collected, good as new, they make it possible to get a rough idea of what might be called a stylistic analysis of Valentino or at least a culling out of certain constant features and predilections that appear throughout his work.

For example, Valentino rejected the fabrics used in the sixties, such as the stiff woolens and chenilles, because they created an abstract outline, a vague geometry of the ordinary, sculpting as well as hindering the way one moved, providing a shell or a shield. Instead, he remained faithful to cloudlike fabrics, to the fluidity and suppleness of the material: crepe georgette, wool crepe, muslin, silk, cashmere, velvet, soft tweeds, jerseys. Missing or infrequent — because, he says, of a lack of imagination on his part — are satin or taffeta. He saves these for only the most special uses, above all for evening wear, as he still finds their application in other spheres problematic.

Materials that sheathe and cling, that marry and follow the shape of the body and the natural gait. Effects of transparency came next, and the designer loved nothing better than the superimposition of delicate fabrics, offering glimpses of a vague motif. Then came all the variations of the next-to-nothing, the aerial sculptures of the flounces, ruches, fluting, tiny pleats that support an invisible matrix, the accent on the neckline and wrists, and other discrete details. Or the orna-

mental may take full possession of the body, transforming it into a sinuous flower or endowing it with subtle wings. These are the famous pieces made for Brooke Shields and Jackie Onassis, where physique is counterpoint to a serpentine line, a sinuous line that for the ancients symbolized life.

Another recurrent motif since the very outset in Valentino's *oeuvre* is the animal. The tiger, the serpent, the panther, and the ocelot are not merely reduced to their spots and their stripes, but sometimes literally worn on the body of the woman, so that it becomes an undulating metaphor for movement. It is as if the designer were trying to conjure up ancient legends of the demon, the magic otherness of a creature that identifies its place in the shadows.

It is easy to understand how fashion designers notoriously assumed to be indifferent to women, consider their art to be dominated by a fascination with an ephemeral and foreign reality, with an elusive and vertiginous femininity. Most of the time — to the point that it has become an annoying cliché — they profess their interest in this aspect of their work and what a boring prospect it would be to design the gray and stereotyped male fashions. As a British fashion historian said, they would be reduced to the monotone "declension" of the costume, almost ecclesiastical, a formula that was developed at the start of the nineteenth century. Dark and serious, male fashion stems from a desire for social acceptance and a persistant puritanism that has become more lax for its female counterpart.

Valentino created his male line in 1969, a line that later branched out in several directions from young fashions to Haute Couture. His approach to this side of his activity does not jibe with the usual clichés. Instead, he prefers to treat it as if he were any master craftsman or project manager entrusted with a task: it is a challenge to be met. He does not by any means approach it with the iconoclastic delight of some designers. He does not question the traditional formulas, nor does he reject the norms. He does not insist, like a naughty, slightly perverse child, on the underlying issue of male fashion, a matter of conventional roles, which distinguishes it clearly from women's fashion. A thoughtful person might denounce these roles, happily passing over centuries of *habitus* and proclaiming indifference to the historical conditions. In any case, Valentino excludes the man's skirt, bold tank tops, and too ostentatiously sexy necklines.

To the contrary, it is a question of introducing the minimum departure, the variation within the range allowed, the subtle innovation and the detail that can make all the difference in a shirt or suit. The man's collection is just one among the many series of sketches made on a daily basis that in the end give rise to the models shown on the runways. For Valentino, the main areas of innovation lie in the choice of fabric, the shades, the lapel, the cuffs, the width of the shoulders, the jacket length, the inclusion or not of buttons, and so on. It is a seasonal variation whose subtlety itself should reflect the trends of the time or the taste of a moment through the elements that distinguish it from the prior season's.

It seems that it was not so easy to take the plunge into untested waters. The driving force behind it and the encouragement came mainly from the partner who has been entrusted with the entrepreneurial aspects of the business for nearly thirty years now. Giancarlo Giammetti — whether he likes it or not — fills the role of the indispensable administrator and critic. The launch of the monogram, symbol of success, was his doing. The prestige-conferring insignia appeared in a period when the anxious search for status and the impassioned quest for the saving ''logo,'' the small outward sign of wealth, the symbol of belonging to an elite or a worldwide aristocracy, was not yet the rampant phenomenon it is today. Thanks to him Valentino came to be included among those select few who offer shelter to an ever-widening circle of clientele that seeks self-confirmation for its breeding, its tradition.

Giammetti paved the way for the foundation of what were originally whims, aiding in the creation of Valentino Uomo, the children's fashions, the teen lines Miss V and Oliver, accessory lines, and even signed linens and furnishings for

Valentino's little friend Oliver, who in 1987 became the emblem of the prêt-à-porter line for the young.

interiors. While in 1970 his decisions reflected a growth policy and were guided by the constant search for new fields of application and opportunities, today his approach is more ''intensive,'' aimed at establishing and managing a fashion distribution network and a product licensing program, and consolidating rapports with their industrial collaborators. All this is handled in Italian fashion. A small staff, a select group of people linked by an almost familial relationship, which can be passionate, demanding, and slightly anarchic. The hierarchical structure is weaker than the classical business models.

Giammetti's physical bearing and behavior show that he is definitely sovereign and sure of his abilities, but without the need to flaunt it. He is completely frank and outspoken about his opinions, even if this means unleashing havoc, as has already happened on more than one occasion with the mass media. He does not bluff nor try to pass himself off for something that he is not. He has an inquisitive gaze, alert, animated, intensified at times by a touch of malice or moderated by ironic irreverence. He seems essentially to be communicating his determination not to be fooled, his knowledge of the fashion industry inside and out, and how to play the game by respecting its rules but not becoming a

1 Haute Couture. Fall-Winter 1969-70.
Full, snow-leopard-trimmed cape in
beige and brown tweed.
Photo Giampaolo Barbieri.
2 Audrey Hepburn and Luchino
Visconti watching the Spring-Summer
1973 fashion show.
Photo Vittoriano Rastelli.
3 The Seventies. Valentino
in his workshop views an Haute
Couture model.

Pages 38-39
Haute Couture. Fall-Winter 1983-84.
Before the show.
Photo Attilio Concari/Courtesy *Vogue*
© 1983 Edizioni Condé Naste S.p.A.

slave to them. He shares with Valentino the conscientiousness of a craftsman whose primary concern is to see a given job well done and the tendency to view commercial success, the ability to satisfy a customer or a given demand, as the only key to true success.

These shared ideas and trajectories explain why he is the only one today, he says, who can speak his mind even about the work of the *couturier,* to bring it in line with a reality that goes beyond the product of the imagination. He plays the role, even when it is painful, of the critic who sometimes corrects a detail of an article to make it meet the public's expectations.

With a gaze that is at once friendly and detached, provocative and critical, Giammetti fills the role of leader and partner. Even his office — where one finds an enigmatic Capogrossi juxtaposed with furniture finished in horn and objects of oriental taste — reflects the pragmatic in its fundamental eclecticism. The essential task reduced to a minimum is to remove all obstacles and problems from the work of the *couturier*, to magnanimously give him his space.

Valentino, according to his partner, is a creator more of lifestyles than of mere fashion trends. The articles of clothing that he designs are just pieces in a puzzle that reflect the rest of his universe. And Rome still remains the center of that universe despite the objections, the occasional sense of confinement and conflict, even moody flights which on the part of either Valentino or Giammetti. We might cite the famous occasion on which the latter hurled invective about the demimondaines and fading actresses who in his opinion overshadowed the capital's "respectable" society. This small incident resulted in the decision to transfer the *defilés* to Paris, fashion capital of the world by all rights. Nevertheless, they did not abandon the banks of the Tiber, choosing instead to put new life into the Palazzo Mignanelli, installing ateliers and workshops, and later opening the *Accademia* wing. No sooner had this been done than it came time to express indignation against the noxious fumes of a symbol of modern consumerism.

Surely, it must be difficult to avoid a feeling of nostalgia for his initial years, and Valentino is sentimentally attached to the small space that stands between via Condotti and via Gregoriana. But there is more to it than this: Rome is clearly a shambles, sooty, vandalized, choked by visual as well as noise pollution, and, paradoxically, by a hopelessly thick provincialism. It is afflicted by the total ineffectiveness of its management, it shrieks with vulgarity, and is impossible to live in, as those who have left it to live in its outskirts will attest.

But Rome continues to be a rainbow of color, a rose of singular nuances, as unique as Venice or Paris. Its infinitely varying harmonies within a given scale nourished the palette of the Scuola Romana painters whose work Valentino and Giammetti so avidly collect. Ocher, red ocher, sienna, yellows, saffrons, brick or oxblood reds, colors of plaster corroded by time, infinite *sfumature*, a hypnotic richness. Perhaps these ubiquitous traces, these scars left by the action of the sun are what give rise to the visitor's first impression of a city in slow motion, slightly hindered, and burdened by the heat that rises from the pavement, as well as by a historical destiny that caused it imperceptibly to drift away from the centers of business. It is a sleep-

ing city, says Valentino, where the withdrawal, the drowsiness, could not be better suited to his work, and this strengthens his determination to stay.

From Gstaad to London to New York, of all the places where it would be possible for Valentino to live, there is one place he mentions with a twinge of regret because he never has the time to go there — Harry's Bar in Venice. It is an exemplary space because it celebrates the art of living in its every smallest detail. A tiny skiff of blond wood docked securely across the canal from the Salute; a *ridotto* whose screened windows and impassive door give no hint of the elegance within; a legendary place consecrated by years of notoriety and *habitués* who became famous in their own right. The extreme restraint of the décor immediately declares its function as a simple setting for a meeting or a conversation. Its culinary offerings are also simple, and in their exquisite freshness have become a paradigm of excellence. It is Venetian cuisine at its best, with its delicate flavors and quantities, discrete mélanges, subtle inventions. It is *bellini* with their incomparable texture, marrying the smooth density of the white peach with the ''spirit'' of *spumante*. The entire aesthetic of Harry's Bar takes in the simplest things and plays off what is sophisticated about them; this gesture of exquisite restraint skims off just the patina, and that is an art.

''I swear that it is extremely difficult for me to understand the souls of men who do not care about objects and about their homes,'' wrote Mario Praz, adding hyperbolically that ''about those who take no interest in their interior decoration, who are unmoved before the harmony of a beautiful piece of furniture, I hold the same opinion as Shakespeare did about people deprived of a musical sense: they are born for betrayal, deceit and theft. The movements of their souls are as somber as the night, their desires as black as Erebus.''

Obviously, Valentino is exempt from the implications of this diatribe, meticulous as he is in the choice of the shades in each of his rooms and their progressive definition. Incidentally, it is curious to note how the fashion designers of today, endlessly shuttled between continents, excel in their mania for the home. Among those who are privileged enough to make their nests in several cities, almost forced to make a show of so many cleverly laid out little boxes, are Valentino, Lagerfeld, and Saint Laurent.

An Italian writer of this century wrote that the pursuit of objects is the passionate longing for pieces of reality that lack a heart, but watch us grow old and imperceptibly take possession of us. Objects that may have been overlooked, just barely missed, and desired all the more for this, calmly witness such violence from a safe distance. They are also, insists Valentino, like so many snapshots of the evolution of an aesthetic that can only gain in intensity, leaving far behind so many errors and so much waste.

Opulence is the key word of his universe. This opulence is represented by the symmetrical arrangements of the large Delft vases (from which he got the inspiration for a collection) on the hearth of Palazzo Mignanelli. Harking back to the reign of William and Mary these structures of porcelain were erected many summers ago inside a chimney hearth. Hanging behind the designer's desk is another example of this luxury, represented by the marble portrait of Eleonora de Toledo by Bronzino, companion to that in the Uffizi.

Eclectic, colorful, and sumptuous, the Roman villa's salon mingles cashmere with petit point, an Empire sofa and a collection of *cloisonnés*, an oriental lacquered screen and a rococo clock; the library with its padded armchairs and Wedgwood vases juxtaposes a huge Botero with a flowery chintz. Throughout the home the Italian baroque style is blended with *cloisonné* objects and chinoiserie cabinets, fine inlay work set alongside Napoléon III *papier mâché* furniture and gilt woodwork with the scrawls of Dufy, Miró, and Picasso.

Furniture, porcelain objects, flowers, fabrics, though belonging to the lexicon of the superfluous, none of these things leaves Valentino indifferent. Because to him, it is clear that humanity is made up of the most gratuitous as well as the most extravagant emotions.

''Frightfully immaculate,'' wrote an Anglo-Saxon journalist one day when faced with a hieratic Valentino seated with a perfectly upright posture, and corresponding in every way to his ideal of the *soigné*.

And though he might be fully immersed in his work, he never lets on. He tackles his job without pathos, without dramas, without creative blocks or a neurotic need to innovate; rather, he is a typical northern Italian who has a marked sense of duty and the desire to see a job well done.

He gets to work early in the morning and starts making sketches: there are ten collections to be drawn and each element must be carefully studied. He chooses color and fabrics, following meetings with textile manufacturers (where the designer makes his suggestions about fabric weights, print designs, materials).

This is a fundamental decision because it orients the design, opening up or clos-

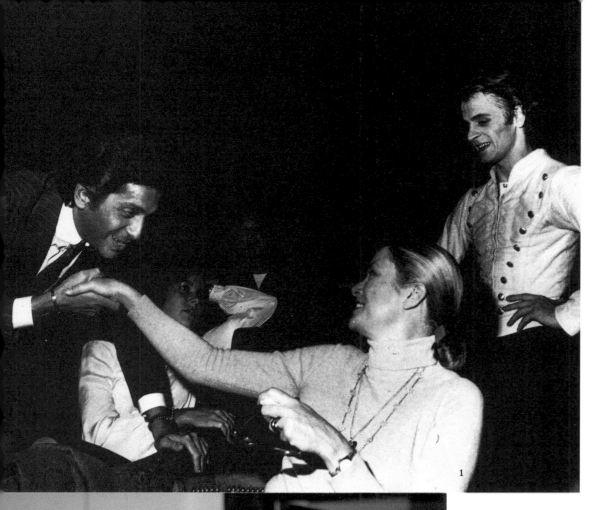

ing off given possibilities of cut and volume. It might also explain why Valentino does not proceed by categorical lines — couture, prêt-à-porter, young fashions — but rather by type of clothing article, conceiving a hundred different suits and then moving on to daytime dresses, sports clothing, overcoats. Then he decides which line they will be part of according

Paris, October 1978.
1 Valentino greeting Grace Kelly as Caroline of Monaco and Mikhail Baryshnikov stand by during a dress rehearsal of Roland Petit's *La Dame de Pique* ballet offered at the Champs Elysées Theater by Valentino to present his signature fragrance. Photo Archivio Valentino.

2 Rome, Accademia Valentino, January 1990. Elizabeth Taylor and Valentino at the presentation of L.I.F.E., an AIDS research association. Photo Archivio Valentino.

3 London, April 30, 1990. AIDS CRISIS TRUST charity fashion show at the Savoy Hotel. Giancarlo Giammetti and Valentino greet H.R.H. the Princess of Wales. Photo Archivio Valentino.

to the typology to which each is most suited.

But to create, says Valentino, is to make variations. Of course, one must begin by finding some element, a theme, a motif, a guideline around which an idea can be developed. But the essence of a collection lies in its details. His flexibility ensures that his work cannot be reduced to a series of ''lines.'' Rather, there are a myriad of accents, solutions, themes, and motifs that crop up musically in the course of his thirty years of activity, like leitmotifs. Because it is another definition that Valentino gives to the fashion designer, perhaps the most striking — that of the unassuming scriptwriter, the faceless but everpresent director. He is absorbed in creating the illusion, hanging the decor, making the body into a magnificent decoy, ''creating the scenario for the grand life,'' but then immediately stepping back to contemplate it from a distance like a dramatist well-satisfied with the job he has done, who stops to take just one last glance and then retreats behind the scene.

Patrick Mauriès

Photo Gianni Giansanti/Sygma/Grazia Neri.

Homage

Thanks to Her Royal Highness Begum Salimah Aga Khan, Her Highness Princess Saddudrin Aga Khan, Her Highness Princess Yasmine Aga Khan, Mrs Gianni Agnelli, Fanny Ardant, Brooke Astor, Lauren Bacall, Mrs Pietro Barilla, Mrs Sid Bass, Marisa Berenson, Mrs Morris Bergreen, Milva Biolcati, Betsy Bloomingdale, Anna Bonomi Bolchini, Florinda Bolkan, Countess Alessandro Bonacossa, Mrs Carlo Bonomi, Mrs Gianmarco Moratti Brichetto, Doris Brynner, Mrs Richard Buckley, Mrs Nicola Bulgari, Duchess Jimmy de Cadaval, Claudia Cardinale, Mrs Franco Carraro, Mrs Antoine Cattan, Mrs Vittorio Cecchi Gori, Ann Cox Chambers, Mrs Jacques Chirac, Countess Donina Cicogna, Countess Marina Cicogna, Mrs Gustavo Cisneros, Joan Collins, Mrs Bettino Craxi, Countess Consuelo Crespi, Pilar Crespi, Duchess Maria Emma d'Acquarone, Countess Brando Brandolini d'Adda, Countess Ruy Brandolini d'Adda, Mrs Marvin Davis, Isa Parodi Delfino, Mimosa Parodi Delfino, Mrs Cicci De Franceschini, Princess Domietta del Drago, Countess Niccolò Donà delle Rose, Vivien Duffield, Doris Duke, Mrs Ahmet Ertegun, Gemma Fabbri, Mrs Giorgio Falck, Rossella Falk, Mrs Amintore Fanfani, Farrah Fawcett, Trini Fierro, Maya Flick, Donatella Flick, Jane Fonda, Mrs Henry Ford, Aretha Franklin, Princess Diane von Fürstenberg, Princess Ira von Fürstenberg, Mrs Marco Gambazzi, Mrs Lorenzo Vallarino Gancia, Mrs Gordon Getty, Mrs Gualtiero Giori, Mrs Alexander Goulandris, Mrs Basile Goulandris, Katharine Graham, Bettina Graziani, Mrs Giorgio Griffa, Mrs John Gutfreund, Mrs Paul Hallingby, Mrs Rafik Hariri, Kathlean Hearst, Veronica Hearst, Muriel Hemingway, Barbara Hendricks, Audrey Hepburn, Anjelica Huston, Lauren Hutton, Mrs Romeo Invernizzi, Glenda Jackson, Eunice Johnson, Her Royal Highness Princess Firyal of Jordan, Her Majesty Queen Noor of Jordan, Mrs Adnan Kashoggi, Mrs Thomas Kempner, Mrs Henry Kissinger, Irith Landeau, Jessica Lange, Estée Lauder, Mary Wells Lawrence, Mrs Giovanni Leone, Tatiana Liberman, Renate Linsenmeyer, Virna Lisi, Gina Lollobrigida, Sophia Loren, Countess Marina Orsi Mangelli, Conchita March, Mrs John Marion, Mrs Zubin Mehta, Mariangela Melato, Liza Minnelli, Mrs Roger Moore, Mrs Robert Mosbacher, Countess Guglielmo Mozzoni, Ornella Muti, Jacqueline Onassis, Her Imperial Highness Farah Pahlavi, Marina Palma, Beatriz Patino, Mrs Rinaldo Piaggio, Paloma Picasso, Princess Luciana Pignatelli, Baroness Ricky di Portanova, Mona Rashid, Countess Jean-Charles of Ravenel, Simonetta Ravizza, Nancy Reagan, Annette Reed, Countess Edouard of Ribes, Marquise Mia de Riencourt, Marisa Monti Riffeser, Hélène Rochas, Rita Rodriguez, Mrs Stefano Romanazzi, Mrs Jean Marie Rossi, Countess Gregorio Rossi di Montelera, Baroness David de Rothschild, Baroness Edmond de Rothschild, Baroness Guy de Rothschild, Mrs Howard Ruby, Mrs Mortimer Sackler, Mrs Edmond Safra, Lucia Moreira Salles, Noorma Sarofim, Her Royal Highness Princess Maria Gabriella of Savoia, Her Royal Highness Princess Marina of Savoia, Mrs Sao Schlumberger, Evelina Shapira, Brooke Shields, Mrs Luigi Sodi, Her Majesty Queen Sofia of Spain, Elena Talenti, Mrs Alfred Taubman, Elizabeth Taylor, Princess Zourab Tchkotoua, Princess Johannes von Thurn und Taxis, Baroness Denise von Thyssen-Bornemisza, Fiona von Thyssen-Bornemisza, Mrs Samir Traboulsi, Ornella Vanoni, Mrs Tony Mayrink Veiga, Veruschka, Monica Vitti, Linda J. Wachner, Baroness Gerald of Waldner, Sigourney Weaver, Raquel Welch, Mrs Michel David Weill, Her Serene Highness Princess Ugo Windisch-Graetz, Jane Wrightsman, and Lynn Wyatt.

Haute Couture. Spring-Summer 1972.
Elizabeth Taylor with Richard Burton at the Bal Proust at Guy de Rothschild's
Château Férrières. The actress wears a black taffeta dress with vertical inserts
of Valenciennes lace and a plunging neckline with ruches in a late
nineteenth-century style. Headpiece made of diamonds and emeralds.
Photo Cecil Beaton/Courtesy Sotheby's.

Pages 48
Haute Couture. Fall-Winter 1969-70.
Audrey Hepburn with black organdy cape.
Photo Giampaolo Barbieri.

Pages 52-53
Haute Couture. Fall-Winter
1967-68.
A photograph of Jacqueline
Onassis during her official visit
to Cambodia. Green toga
trimmed with pearl
and crystal beads.
Photo Archivio Valentino.

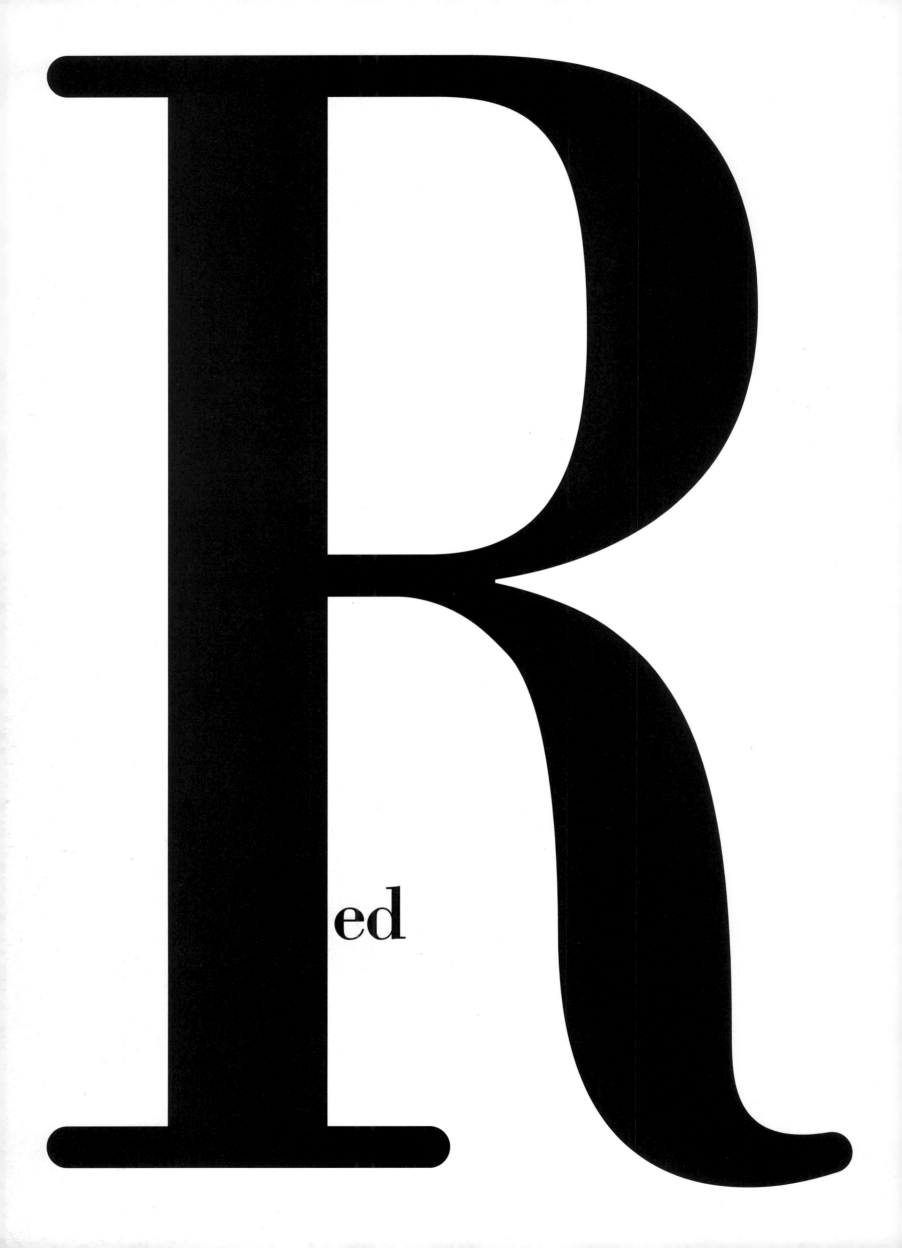

66Why so much red? Perhaps because I was born under the sign of Taurus? In any case, red is a bewitching color, standing for life, blood, and death, passion, love, and an absolute remedy for sadness and gloom. I remember one of the most striking impressions I ever had in my life: it was in Barcelona, when I was a student. I'd been invited by a friend of mine to the opera where with fascination I beheld, in a box, a very beautiful grey-haired woman dressed in red velvet from head to toe. Amid all the colors worn by the women, she appeared to me to be unique, standing out in all her splendor. I have never forgotten her. For me she became the red goddess. Something fabulous. I think a woman dressed in red is always magnificent. In the middle of a crowd, she is the quintessence of the heroine. Diana Vreeland continues to be for me the greatest heroine of all times. She had an acute sense of things, of true fashion. She had an infallible critical eye. She knew better than anybody else the meaning of the word *allure*; she was also a great journalist. And then, she also adored the color red; her apartment was completely *rouge*. Unique!99

Rome, Via Gregoriana.
1960. Valentino in his atelier with highlights of red in the décor.
Photo Team/Grazia Neri.

Prêt-à-porter. Fall-Winter 1988-89.
Paris. ''Ecological'' fake fur in ''Valentino red.''
Photo Robert Frankenberg/*Marie-Claire* © Mondadori Press.

Valentino red.   **1** Haute Couture. Fall-Winter 1984-85. Evening gown with long sleeves and asymmetrical drapery.
2 Haute Couture. Spring-Summer 1985. Evening gown with low-cut back, clinging fit, and two black taffeta bow accents.
3 Haute Couture. Spring-Summer 1983. Pleated and long-fringed evening gown.
Photos Janos Grapow/Archivio Valentino.

Valentino red.   1 Haute Couture. Spring-Summer 1989. Slinky evening gown with asymmetrical neckline and short, draped petal-sleeve.
2 Haute Couture. Fall-Winter 1984-85. Slinky evening gown with vertical drapery and fitted sleeves.
3 Haute Couture. Fall-Winter 1987-88. Evening gown in damask fabric with black ribbon insert ending in a large bow.
Photos Janos Grapow/Archivio Valentino.

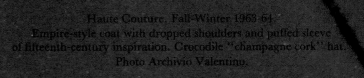

Haute Couture, Fall-Winter 1963-64.
Empire-style coat with dropped shoulders and puffed sleeve
of fifteenth-century inspiration. Crocodile "champagne cork" hat.
Photo Archivio Valentino.

Captions on page 329.

"In fantasy color becomes a story, a succession of images. When that color is red and the image is created by clothing" the storyteller is Valentino. The article of clothing in red — or better, in "Valentino red" — is something more than a way of telling a story: it is synonymous with style and therefore out of the ordinary. Red is a constant feature of Valentino's fashions, a note that is not only chromatic, but a flash of great allure, of elegant seduction. Each time it appears, Valentino red is like a lietmotif in the continuing symphony of each of his défilés. Contemporary, timeless, infinitely varied, Valentino red undergoes a process of self-detachment. Valentino red is a given fact, a reality outside of current events; it is closer to the idea of the myth. Valentino explains: "I started to fall in love with this color during my first visit to Barcelona when I was seventeen years old. A friend took me to the opera; it was the start of the season. The women perched in the boxes around me seemed to be a garland of red flowers. They all wore something in red, and it struck me. That image came back to me when I started designing." The memory can be traced back to one of the first dresses that a very young Valentino designed for a famous friend when he was still in the atelier of Jean Dessès in Paris. The line was romantic, conceived for an elegant figure, where the red is exalted by the play of transparency, the contrast between lustrous and matte, with ribbon and knot motifs. This elegant evening gown already shows the essence of Valentino's style: a style that never ceases to astonish, to amaze, though it still respects the rules of the game. It is a classical look that harks

back to various canons. In-ative needs, the rigorously other more opulent, baroque role is played by the selection values in a sort of eclecticism the present and the illusion of craftsmanship blended with yields stunning results. We color; it is synonymous with the symbol of strength and rousing, and contagious. Red colors, and one that most always had strong, though at values, representing love, but iconography red stands for ed to martyrdom, but its to become in medieval paint-the color of the demon. Red interpretation of such folklore Hood," where it stands tion. With Valentino, red is poppies which are a recurrent he uses. This flower's petals are in his creations; they can be blown by the wind, an ethere-chiffon. Each era has recur-aesthetic, becoming metaphors, and ambiguities; all this sur-

Fernando Botero, *Femme habillée en Valentino*.
Oil on canvas, 47 × 40 in.
Rome, Valentino Garavani collection.

Page 69
Haute Couture. Fall-Winter 1988-89.
Evening dress in red crepe and chiffon, classical line.
Photo Walter Chin/Archivio Valentino.

novating in response to cre-composed styles alternate with styles where a fundamental of a fabric with the right ranging between the world of the past. The unquestionable the study of detail always know that red is a stimulating warmth and energy; it is also passion; it is eye-catching, is one of the three primary lends itself to *sfumato*. It has times contradictory, symbolic also violence. In Christian spiritual greatness often link-ambivalent nature enabled it ing a symbol of the inferno, can be a disturbing key to the classics as "Little Red Riding between innocence and seduc-also the red of his favorite motif in the print fabrics a pretext, a point of departure transformed into a dress al material such as voile or rent images that reflect its allegories, embodying utopias faces in the images of the pe-

riod's "fashion." An example is Valentino red; in fact, "lovers of consummate beauty," aesthetes, elegant people of culture appreciate the message of Valentino red, especially in our times of colorful though insistent messages. Discerning the beauty of "detail," avoiding "conspicuous waste," and giving rise to sensations that stand out for the quality and subtlety of their formal rigor — this is beauty for beauty's sake, a complete abstraction. Red is red because it is Valentino.

Bonizza Giordani Aragno

Haute Couture. Spring-Summer 1981.
Brooke Shields wearing red organdy evening gown inspired by Botero's
Femme habillée en Valentino.
Photo Dick Ballarian/Courtesy *Harper's Bazaar Italia.*

1989. Jewelry, eyeglasses, gloves, and stole.
Photo Gary Deane.

Page 73
Valentino red rose.
Photo Russel Lamb.

Rome

66Rome is unique: a city where one should not work, but only walk about, seeing the sights and discovering new things all the time. It's a city that takes my breath away. When in Rome, one should take the opportunity to experience the *Ponentino*, at that magical hour between day and night, when gentle relaxation at last takes over. It is a city of

lights, of colors. For thirty years, Rome and I are sharing a never-ending passion. She is a delicious lover who makes us feel that we, too, are eternal.**99**

Haute Couture. Spring-Summer 1972.
Valentino at the Imperial Forum.
Photo Herbert Rowan/Archivio Valentino.

Page 75
Rome. View of the Imperial Forum under a blanket of snow.
Photo Isidoro Genovese.

Page 77
Haute Couture. Fall-Winter 1984-85.
Draped black velvet dress with black jersey jacket. Fur cuffs and hat.
Photo Arthur Elgort/Courtesy *Vogue* © 1984 Edizioni Condé Nast S.p.A.

Haute Couture. Spring-Summer 1976.
An encounter between baroque architecture and fashion
in Rome's Piazza del Popolo. Wool chain-printed coat.
Photo Regi Relang. Courtesy Verlag Hans
Schöner © *30 Jahre Mode Italien*.

Page 79
Haute Couture. Fall-Winter 1984-85.
Evening dress with draped bodice in pink silk jersey
and a matching silk skirt in Rome's via Condotti.
Photo Mark Arbeit/*Moda*.

Haute Couture. Spring-Summer 1980.
Black crepe evening dress with large white taffeta bow.
Photo Alberta Tiburzi.

Page 81
Haute Couture. Spring-Summer 1980.
Yellow crepe de chine evening gown
with matching taffeta bow.
Rome, Monument to the Unknown Soldier.
Photo Alberta Tiburzi.

1985.
Valentino celebrates twenty-five years
of fashion with his Haute Couture
seamstresses on Piazza di Spagna's steps.
Photo Jean-Pierre Goudeaut.

Page 82
Haute Couture. Fall-Winter 1987-88.
Red evening gown with asymmetrical hem
and large black bow on Ara Coeli's steps.
Photo Cristina Ghergo.

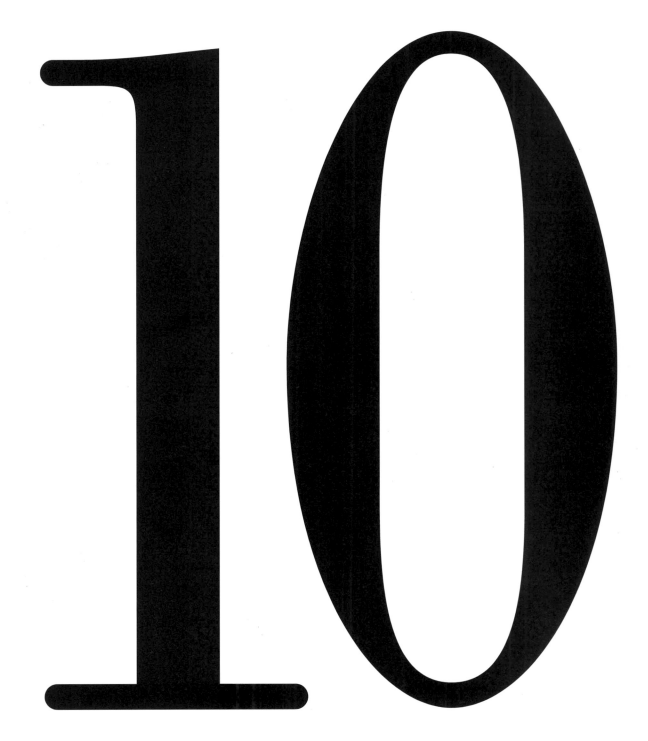

The first

10

years

rotosei
settimanale

Rossana Podestà nell'atelier del sarto
Valentino (Servizio alle pagine 48-51)

66 *1960* was the great year when there was born in me a feeling of boundless enthusiasm, an unfurling of joys and passions. I felt the exaltation that everyone feels on the threshold of a career; in those days I would conceive a thousand ideas a second, and in a year I could have set up 400 collections. It was a period of profuse, uncontrolled imagination in all directions, reflecting a limitless creative appetite. *1970*, on the other hand,

marked a phase that I never really liked. It was a period of exaggeration in which, like everyone else, I had a share, but one of no historical interest. If I were to be frank, I would say that it was a period I should prefer to forget, erase from my mind. It was a period of non-fashion. On the other hand, I adore my fashions of the years 1971-76, when they returned to being beautiful, simple, free from excess or constraint. **99**

Captions on page 329.

Captions on page 329.

Belle de jour

❝When I dream of preparing my collection, my immediate thought is of an evening dress; if the concept of work comes into the picture, then I think of a daytime outfit. That's because it's much easier to imagine a woman walking across a ballroom than an active type who has to get through the whole working day and emerge triumphant. The daytime part of a collection calls for a lot of technical research; it's a very important part because it represents the hallmark, the essential character of a fashion parade. The 'Belle de Jour' has to be even more remarkable because hers is an environment of less artifice. The daytime beauty needs to display her self-confidence unflaggingly for a great many hours on end. That's why I feel it's up to me to give her a carefree image. **❞**

Page 95
Haute Couture. Fall-Winter 1983-84.
Wool houndstooth jacket with asymmetrical lapels over a black velvet dress; small toque with feather.
Photo Horst P. Horst/Courtesy *Vogue* © 1983 Edizioni Condé Nast S.p.A.

Page 96
Prêt-à-porter. Spring-Summer 1970.
Blue wool redingote over blue-and-white printed silk dress.
Photo Oliviero Toscani/Archivio Valentino.

Prêt-à-porter. Fall-Winter 1990-91.
Pink wool coat cinched at waist with a small self-belt.
Photo Michel Comte/Courtesy *Vogue* © 1990 The Condé Nast Publications Ltd.

Haute Couture. Spring-Summer 1985.
Pink wool jacket with double row of black buttons.
Photo Stan Malinowsky.

Haute Couture. Fall-Winter 1963-64.
Pink wool suit with bow at waist;
jaguar hat.
Photo Archivio Valentino.

Prêt-à-porter. Fall-Winter 1990-91.
Short pink wool coat with jewel neckline.
Photo Patrick Demarchelier/Courtesy *Vogue*
© 1990 Edizioni Condé Nast S.p.A.

Haute Couture. Fall-Winter 1966-67.
Trouser suit in tweed wool; fur and fabric hat.
Photo Helmut Newton/Courtesy *Vogue* © 1966 Edizioni Condé Nast S.p.A..

Prêt-à-porter. Fall-Winter 1981-82.
White spencer with black velvet buttons
and collar; black trousers.
Photo Claus Wickrath/*Donna*.

Page 102
Haute Couture. Spring-Summer 1990.
Ivory-colored wool suit with ''pagoda'' hat.
Photo Mario Testino/Courtesy
Harpers & Queen Magazine.

Prêt-à-porter. Fall-Winter 1988-89.
Blue shantung dress with white lapels
and large buttons down the middle.
Photo David Bailey/Courtesy *Vogue*
© 1988 Edizioni Condé Nast S.p.A.

Haute Couture. Fall-Winter 1965-66.
Op-striped blue-and-white suit with
solid-color collar and pockets.
Photo Archivio Valentino.

Haute Couture. Fall-Winter 1987-88.
Seven-eighths camel hair coat.
Photo Giampaolo Barbieri.

Fall-Winter 1989-90.
Miss V suit. Eyeglasses by Valentino.
Photo Peter Hönnemann/*L'Officiel*.

1 Haute Couture. Fall-Winter 1987-88. Red cashmere redingote edged in sable. Photo Vittoriano Rastelli/Archivio Valentino.   2 Haute Couture. Fall-Winter 1985-86. Quilted jacket with fur trim. Photo Terence Donovan/Archivio Valentino.   3 Prêt-à-porter. Fall-Winter 1989-90. Blue spencer over a gray quilted skirt open in front; blouse with lace collar, reminiscent of the nineteenth century. Photo Walter Chin/Archivio Valentino.   4 Haute Couture. Fall-Winter 1963-64. Shocking pink wool suit. Photo AIS.   5 Prêt-à-porter. Fall-Winter 1987-88. Black suit with velvet collar and jewelry by Valentino. Photo Steven Meisel/Archivio Valentino.   6 Haute Couture. Fall-Winter 1988-89. Brown suit with pleated skirt, blouson-style jacket with broad collar and cuffs in fur, man's-style hat. Photo David Bailey/Archivio Valentino.

Haute Couture. Fall-Winter 1990-91.
Jersey suit and quilted waistcoat, longline jacket,
earrings, and high boots all in pink.
Photo Patrick Demarchelier/Courtesy *Vogue*
© 1990 Edizioni Condé Nast S.p.A.

Haute Couture. Fall-Winter 1983-84.
Detail of shoe with sole decorated
in Scotch plaid pattern
(by René Caovilla).
Photo Archivio Valentino.

Page 110
Haute Couture. Fall-Winter 1983-84.
Redingote with wide, cartwheel skirt
in black-and-red checked wool; wide
black leather belt and embroidered
buckle; black toque.
Photo Horst P. Horst/Courtesy *Vogue*
© 1983 Edizioni
Condé Nast S.p.A.

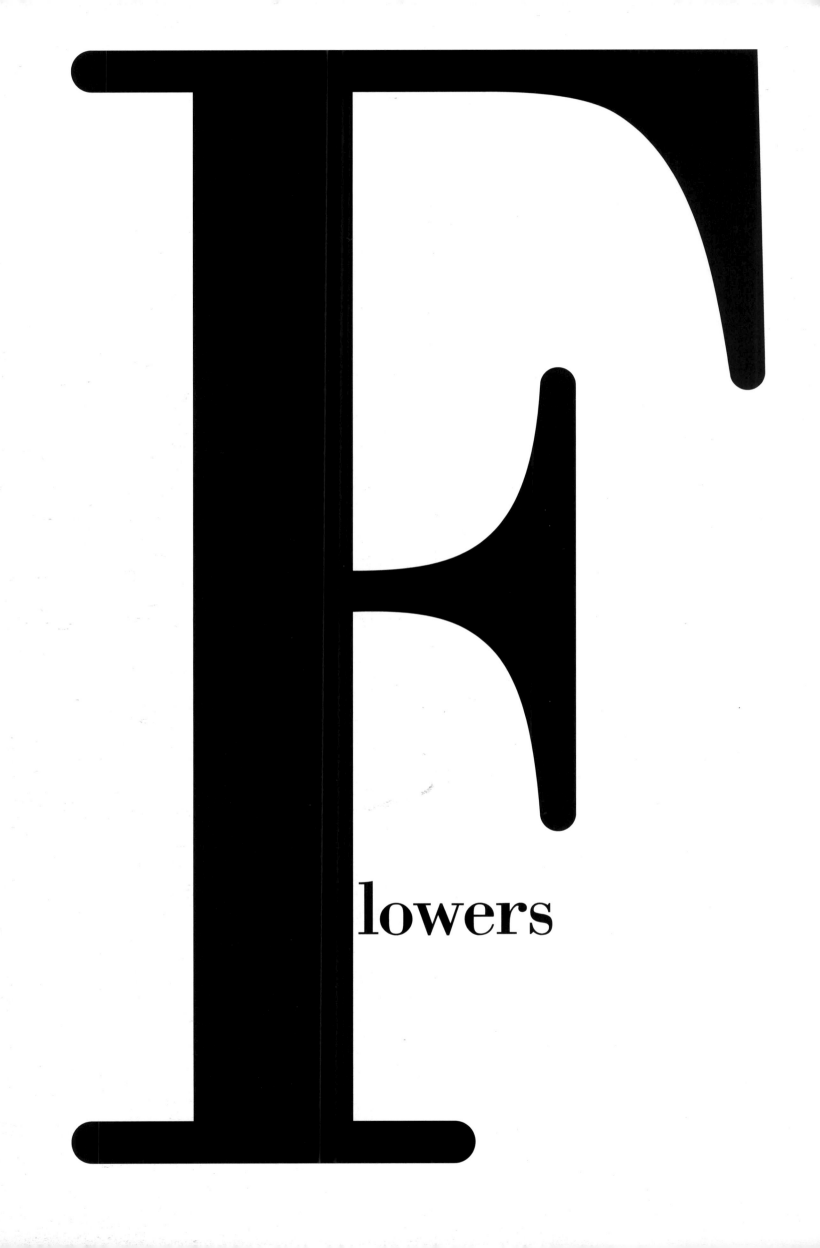

66I shouldn't like to go through life without flowers. I love being surrounded by them; so often, they are a sign of joy. None of my houses can be without them. Sometimes I buy them myself — in fact, one of my greatest pleasures is to go out and buy some at Covent Garden market. Flowers, for me, are a great source of inspiration; I like to reproduce them on a dress, turning a woman into a bouquet. They bring happiness. I have a passion for peonies; I always look for a very big, spectacular one that comes from San Francisco. I think I must be a true collector of these ephemeral works of art. I also like roses, cyclamens, snowballs, pink camellias, and hibiscus. I have paid homage to all these flowers that overwhelm me with their beauty in my creations of fabrics and dresses. **99**

Page 113
Paris, Jardin de Bagatelle.
Photo Alexandre Bailache/Archivio Valentino.

Page 115
Haute Couture. Spring-Summer 1969.
White evening dress with floral motifs embroidered in petit point.
Photo Carlo Orsi.

Pages 116
Detail of bolero with sequin and rhinestone embroidery.
Photo Janos Grapow/Archivio Valentino.

Page 117
Haute Couture. Fall-Winter 1989-90.
Evening dress in flower print satin with flowing satin stole.
Photo Walter Chin/Archivio Valentino.

Cetona, Giancarlo Giammetti's country home:
detail of the winter garden.
Photo Oberto Gili/*House & Garden*

Haute Couture. Spring-Summer 1986.
Flower print dress with draped bodice.
Drawing Michael Meyring.

Page 120
Haute Couture. Spring-Summer 1968.
Organdy dress with embroidered
flowers and pleated cuffs, embroidered
stockings, eighteenth-century-style
shoes with bow.
Photo Regi Relang/Courtesy Verlag
Hans Schöner © *30 Jahre Mode Italien.*

Haute Couture. Spring-Summer 1989.
Victorian-style flower-print silk evening gown with drapery
and ruche trim at the waist and along the edges.
Venice, Museo Fortuny.
Photo Cristina Ghergo/Archivio Valentino.

Black and white

66A woman dressed in black and white is to me like a kind of symbol or a signature. In all my collections I always include a black-and-white item, because it provides a sort of rest in the middle of all the colors. At the same time, this kind of punctuation interrupts and thus strengthens a collection. Black and white is just as much a classic as red or beige. A woman who wears black and white is strong and certain to have a great personality — a woman who knows what she wants. That's the sort of woman I admire. **99**

Page 125
Victor Vasarely, *Helios*, 1960.
Oil, 72 × 86 in.
Paris, Galerie Denise René.

On this page
Haute Couture. Fall-Winter 1989-90.
Black stretch leggings with sweeping black and white satin stole.
Photo Satoshi Saikusa/Courtesy *Vogue* © 1989 Edizioni Condé Nast S.p.A.

Page 127
Haute Couture. Fall-Winter 1967-68.
Veruschka. Palazzo pajama in oversized black polka-dot pattern.
Photo Franco Rubartelli/Courtesy *Vogue* © 1967 Edizioni Condé Nast S.p.A.

Haute Couture. Fall-Winter 1979-30.
Mask inspired by surrealism.
Photo Courtesy *Harper's Bazaar Italia*.

Page 128
Drawing from the book
Ornament zwischen Hoffnung und Verbrechen,
by Josef Hoffmann, Vienna 1987.

Captions on page 329.

Prêt-à-porter. Spring-Summer 1990.
Long, striped sheath-dress in
black-and-white crepe marocain.
Photo Alfa Castaldi/Courtesy *Vogue*
©1990 Edizioni Condé Nast S.p.A.

Spring-Summer 1987.
Black-and-white Valentino accessories.
Photo Gary Deane/Archivio Valentino.

Page 133
Haute Couture. Fall-Winter 1965-66.
Sequined top with op-inspired
geometric motifs.
Photo Janos Grapow/Archivio Valentino.

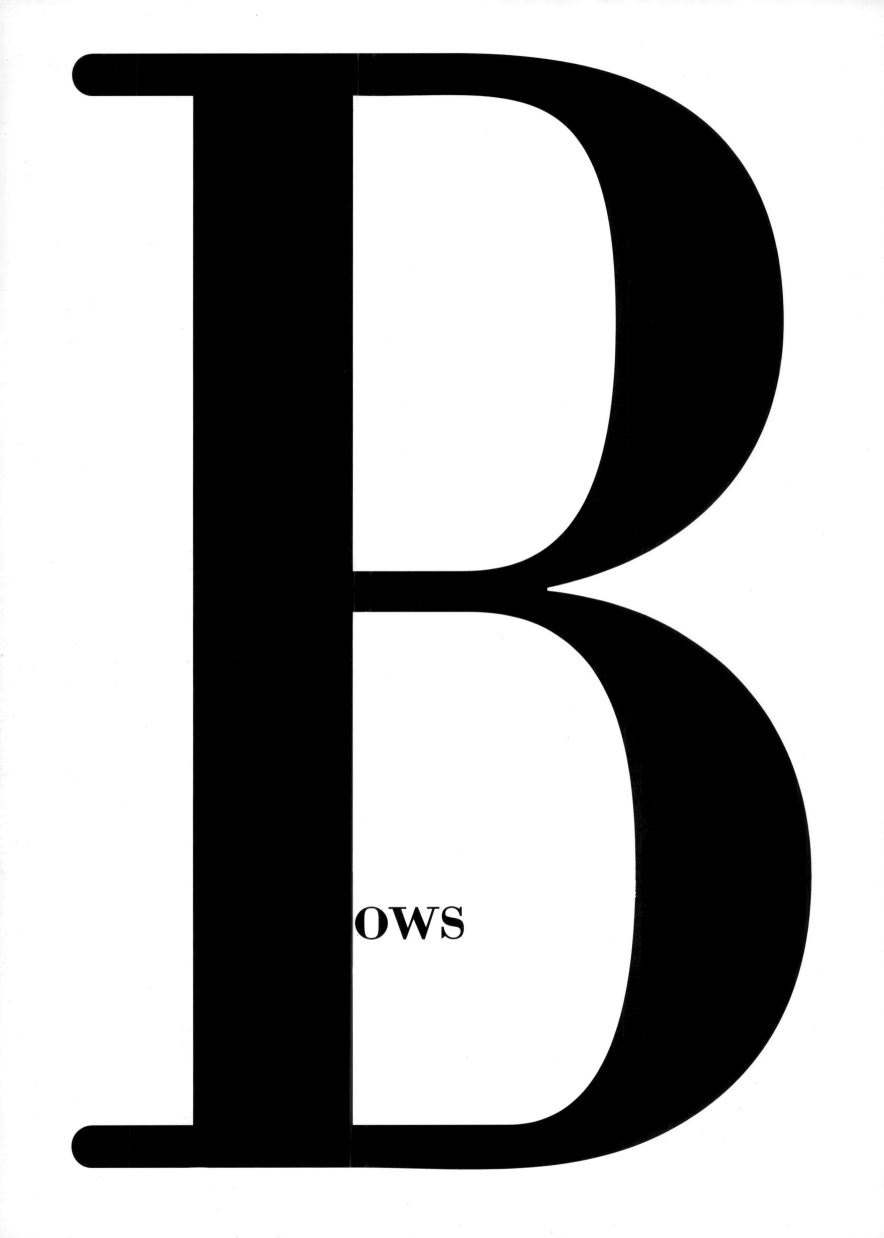

> **66** Bows are an obvious symbol of total femininity. As indispensable as an exclamation point at the end of a phrase, they may be a refined way of marking the spot where draped materials cease to flow. They remind me of one of my favorite models: the famous Dalma who during a fashion parade presented a red dress that ended in a bow. The people clapped for ten minutes, and she dissolved in tears. It was one of my most rewarding moments. **99**

Page 135
Haute Couture. Fall-Winter 1987-88.
Detail of pink satin skirt with ruffle hem and
large bow;
shoes in matching pink satin.
Photo Javier Vallhonrat/Studio Filomeno.

On this page
Haute Couture. Spring-Summer 1980.
Clingy evening gown with drapery and bow
over the shoulders.
Drawing Michael Meyring.

Page 137
Haute Couture. Fall-Winter 1985-86.
Baroque-look bracelet with double bow in gemstones and rhinestones.
Photo Bob Stern.

Haute Couture. Spring-Summer 1983.
Detail of evening dress with large
butterfly bow at the back in
black-and-white printed fabric.
Photo Renato Grignaschi/
Archivio Valentino.

Page 138
Prêt-à-porter. Fall-Winter 1988-89.
Heavy black satin evening dress
with three large white bows.
Photo Walter Chin/Archivio Valentino.

Captions on page 329.

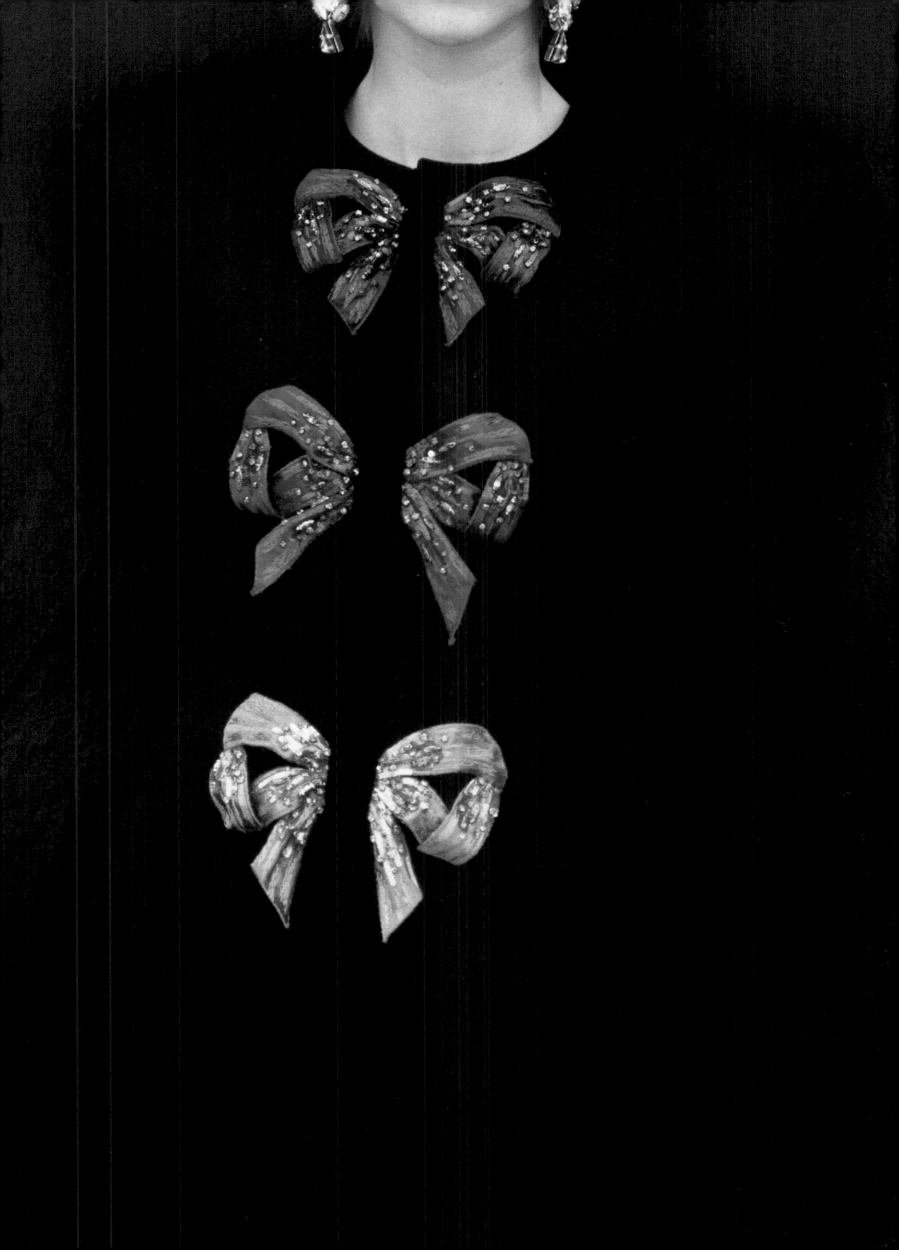

Prêt-à-porter. Fall-Winter 1985-86.
Long red sheath-dress with drapery clasped
by a looped black bow.
Photo Philippe Webb/*L'Officiel*.

Page 141
Haute Couture. Fall-Winter 1989-90.
Detail of black jacket with three embroidered
bows in different colors.
Photo Serge Barbeau/*L'Officiel*.

Page 143
Prêt-à-porter. Fall-Winter 1987-88.
Evening dress with asymmetrical neckline and
drapery clasped by a flat bow at the shoulder.
Photo Nadir.

Prêt-à-porter. Fall-Winter 1987-88.
Black evening gown with pleated underskirt
in the same gold fabric as the looped ribbon.
Photo Nadir/Courtesy *Vogue* © 1987
Condé Nast Verlag GmbH.

Page 145
Haute Couture. Fall-Winter 1982-83.
Richly draped black evening gown with bow clasp
at the waist and a large rose in its center.
Photo Arthur Elgort/Courtesy *Vogue* © 1982
Les Publications Condé Nast S.A.

Captions on page 329.

Prêt-à-porter. Spring-Summer 1980.
Evening gown with oversized bow.
Photo Peter Lindbergh/Courtesy *Vogue*
© 1980 Edizioni Condé Nast S.p.A.

Polka dots

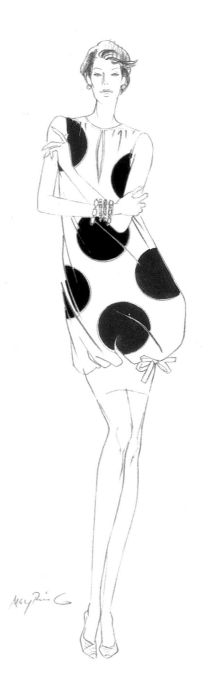

66I like women who wear polka dots: they're always fun and even when they're resting, they seem to be moving. Polka dots are for me a basic tool of my trade like all the other classics: gray flannel, plain jersey, tweeds. A fabric with polka dots can be combined with anything: with floral, check, or striped materials. Yes, I set great store by women who wear polka dots. They denote a sense of lightness, of playfulness, of humor, a certain nonchalance, a taste for racy gaiety. Or simply wit. **99**

Page 149
Haute Couture. Spring-Summer 1988.
Blue-and-white turban.
Photo David Bailey/Archivio Valentino.

On this page
Haute Couture. Spring-Summer 1982.
Bulle dress in oversized polka dots pattern.
Drawing Michael Meyring.

Page 151
Haute Couture. Spring-Summer 1987.
Sheath-dress with white polka dots on black background.
Photo François Halard/Visual Team.

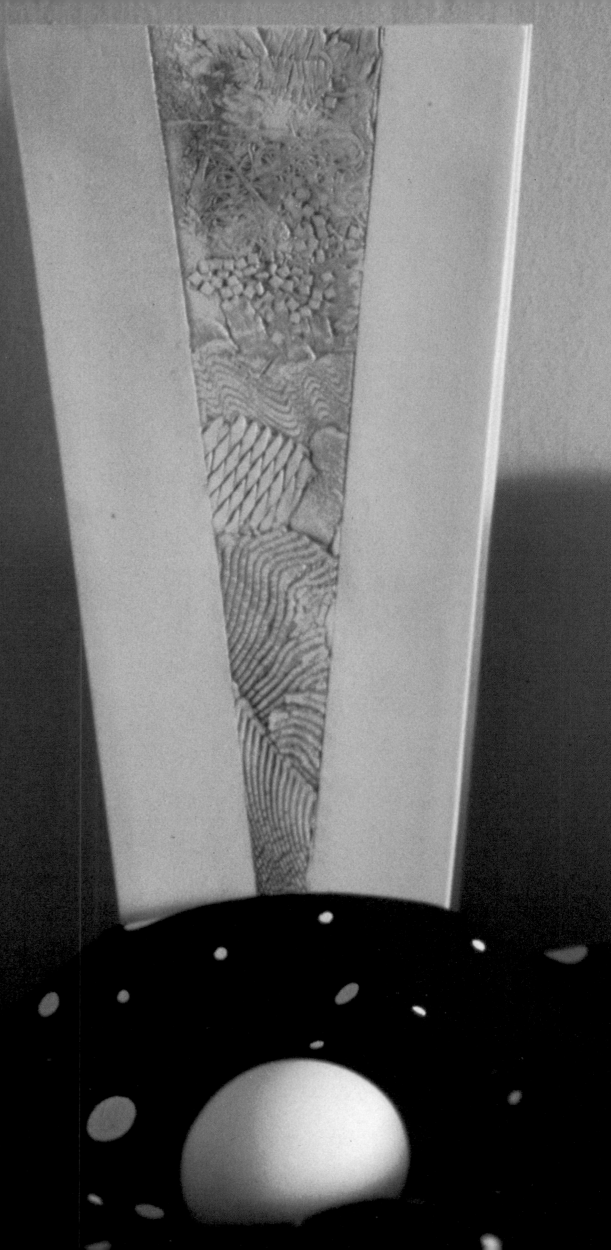

Clutch bag in rigorous geometric lines
with tiny polka dots pattern.
Photo Sheila Metzner/Archivio Valentino.

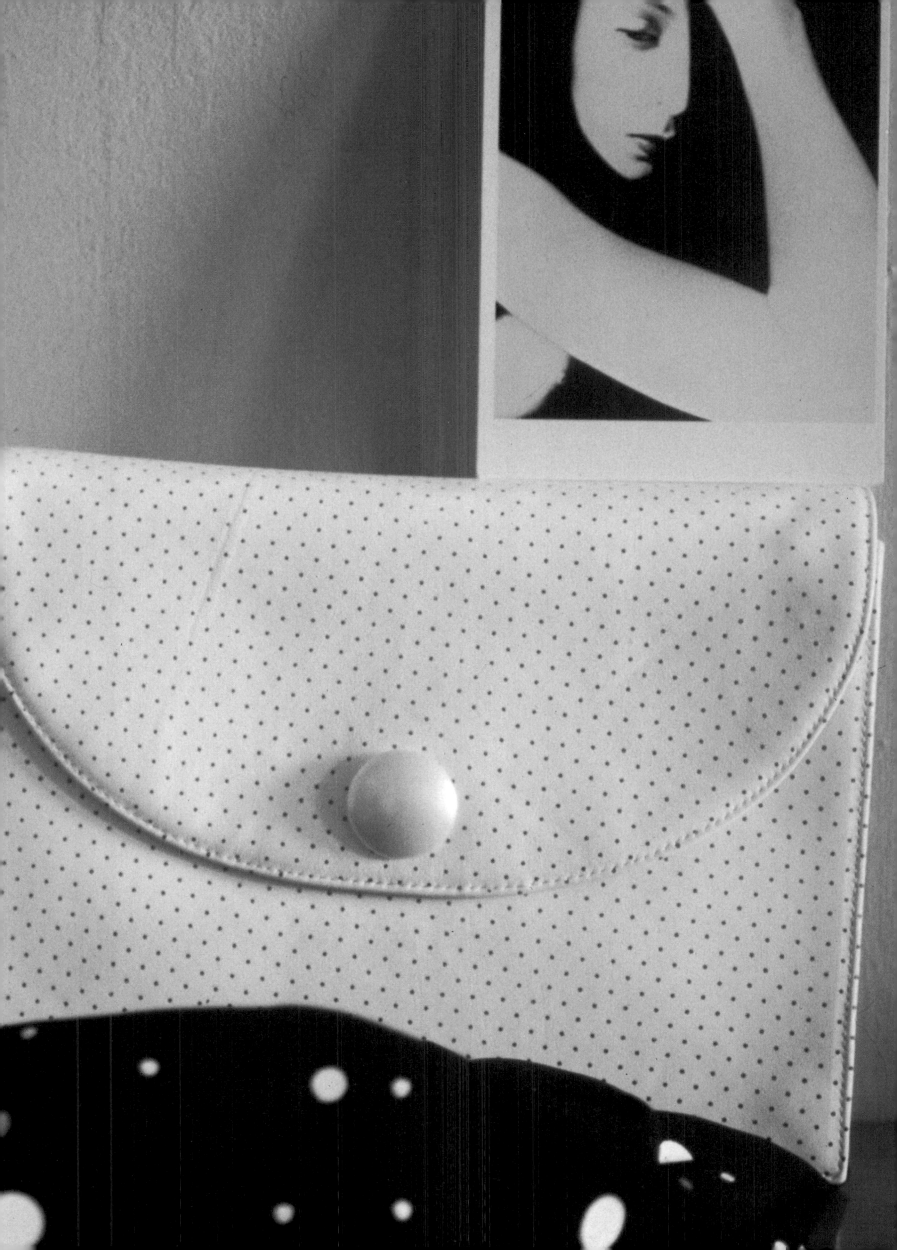

Prêt-à-porter. Spring-Summer 1985.
A galaxy of large and small polka dots
on a tightly fitted dress.
Photo Sheila Metzner/Archivio Valentino.

Haute Couture. Spring-Summer 1988.
Black silk and black-and-white polka-
dot satin evening gown.
Photo David Bailey/*Amica*.

Haute Couture. Spring-Summer 1984.
Evening gown with black and white sequin polka dots.
Photo Alberta Tiburzi.

Haute Couture. Spring-Summer 1983.
Cocktail dress in red crepe with black polka dots.
Photo Helmut Newton/Archivio Valentino.

Captions on page 329-30.

Shoe. 1985.
Polka dots and scalloped edging in classic shoe design.
Photo Jim Reiher/Archivio Valentino.

Prêt-à-porter. Spring-Summer 1987.
Red chiffon dress in red-and-black polka
dots; turban with large bow and black rose.
Photo Lothar Schmidt/Archivio Valentino.

Page 161
Prêt-à-porter. Spring-Summer 1988.
Detail of petal-shaped sleeve in floral
pattern silk
with oversized polka dots.
Photo Courtesy *Harper's Bazaar Italia*.

F rom the sea

66 The sea holds me in its spell almost more than anything else because I find it impossible to resist its infinite, ever-changing beauty. For it has the magic and the strength of the mountains, which are also dear to my heart. I love its many colors, its poetry, and its calm. Mankind should heed and respect it, instead of filling it with all kinds of harmful refuse. **99**

Prêt-à-porter. Spring-Summer 1983.
Bathing suit with large appliqué wave.
Photo Giovanni Gastel/*Donna*.

Page 163
Valentino PIÙ, 1974.
Shell-shaped pillows.
Photo Susan Wood.

Page 165
Valentino 1984.
Draped bathing suit with rhinestone ring.
Photo Helmut Newton/Archivio Valentino.

Pages 166-167
Scipione, *Il risveglio della bionda sirena* (*The Blond Siren's Awakening*), 1929.
Oil on panel, 31½ × 39 in.
(Exhibited at the opening of the Accademia Valentino on January 18, 1990.)
Archivio della Scuola Romana.

Prêt-à-porter. Spring-Summer 1984.
Polka-dot draped bathing suit.
Photo Alberto Dell'Orto/*Moda*.

Page 169
Prêt-à-porter. Spring-Summer 1984.
Bathing suit in lycra with multicolored polka dots.
Photo Sarah Moon.

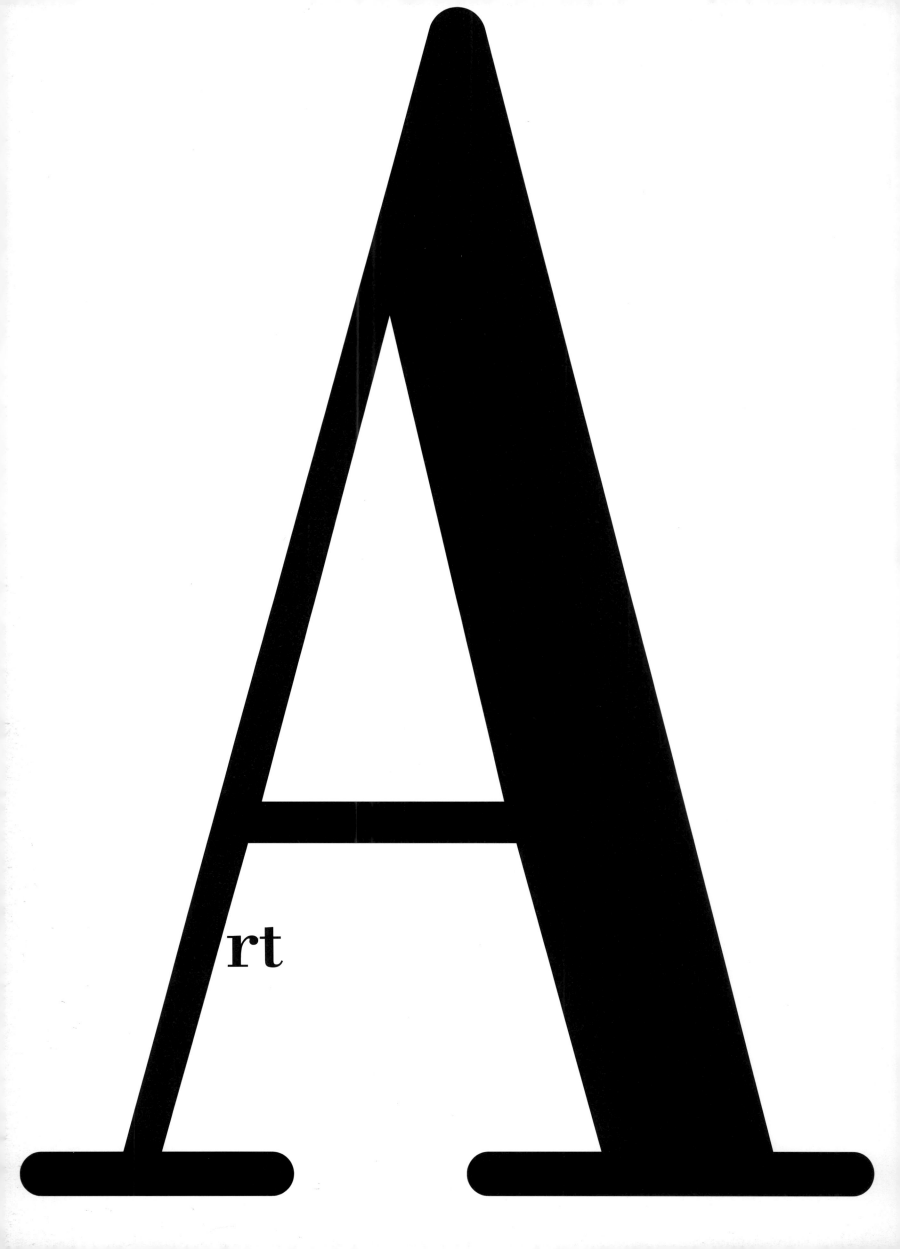

Page 173
Haute Couture. Spring-Summer 1989.
Embroidered bodice, eighteenth-century look.
Photo Janos Grapow/Archivio Valentino.

Page 175
Haute Couture. Spring-Summer 1969.
Dress with fringe and rich embroidery.
Photo Archivio Valentino.

❝I've always been curious. Art — with a capital A — interests me greatly. I can spend hours in museums when I'm on my travels. The museum I like best is perhaps the Rijksmuseum in Amsterdam. I have an unreserved admiration for the great masters: Rembrandt, Velázquez, Goya, Bruegel. I'm also deeply moved by the places where paintings are found, by such imposing objects as the Russian marbles at Leningrad's Hermitage, impressive delftware, the Klimt in the Palais Stoclet in Brussels, and the sobriety of Hoffmann. I am myself a keen collector. Sometimes I imbue a dress with the excitement I felt on seeing certain works of art: for example, my collections have included Russian themes, things by Hoffmann, or Etruscan or Greco-Roman motifs. Art is an inexhaustible source of wealth and joy.**❞**

Page 176
Haute Couture. Spring-Summer 1968.
Ball gown in satin printed with motifs
inspired by Delft pottery.
Photo Henry Clarke/Courtesy *Vogue*
© 1968 Condé Nast Publications Inc.

Page 177
Haute Couture. Fall-Winter 1969-70.
Dress with oriental-inspired decorative motifs
showing Chinese dragons.
Photo Giampaolo Barbieri.

Amphora. Second half of the sixth century B.C.
Black-figured attic vase, height 12 in.
Rome, Museo Nazionale Etrusco di Villa Giulia (formerly Castellani Collection).
Photo Archivio Valentino.

Page 178
Prêt-à-porter. Fall-Winter 1989-90.
Sweater embroidered with motifs inspired by Etruscan pottery.
Photo Janos Grapow/Archivio Valentino.

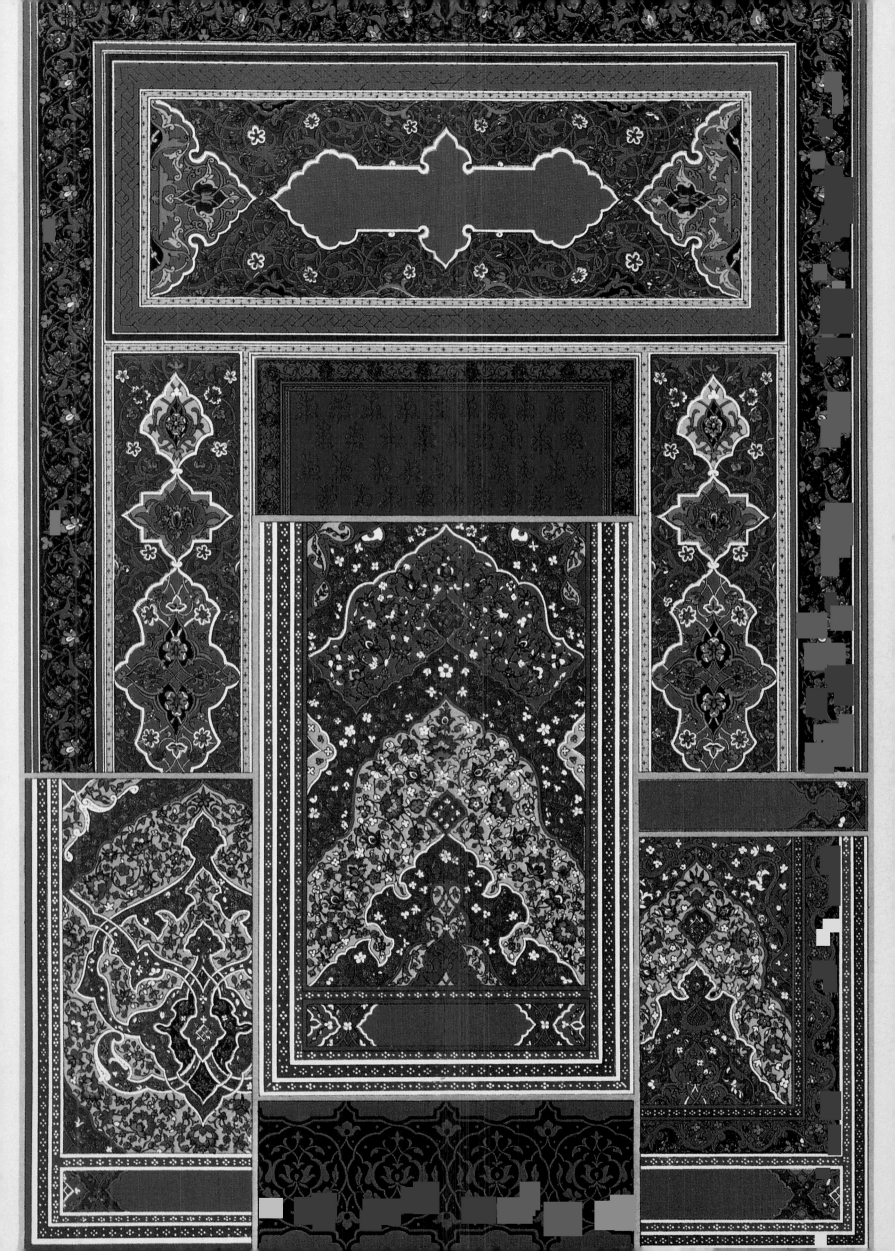

On this page
Prêt-à-porter. Fall-Winter 1989-90.
Treated shearling parka with insets
in a design of Etruscan inspiration.
Photo Janos Grapow/Archivio Valentino.

Page 189
Haute Couture. Spring-Summer 1966.
Palazzo pajama with motifs
of Incan inspiration.
Photo Archivio Valentino.

66 At the start of my career, when fashion houses could take any liberties they pleased, and their rich customers were free to indulge any whim, I used to have the wildest ideas. The time had come to call it to a halt, but no one realized it, and the tiger and the ocelot continued to be hunted with impunity. In those days I used to invent clothes that would be out of the question today: an ermine coat lined with leopard, lynx capes, and the first white mink coat, back in the seventies. Extravagance, whatever the cost, was the order of the day! Neither sable nor chinchilla held any mystery for me. But suddenly we became responsible and had qualms of conscience. With nature and the environment in peril and modern techniques that made it unnecessary, why should we continue the large-scale massacre of animals? What can be the justification for it? As long ago as 1962 I had invented an artificial zebra and in 1965 an artificial crocodile skin, after having created tunics in real crocodile edged with sable. Nowadays we can definitely say that a woman who wears real animal skins is out of place. What's more, artificial furs and skins provide much more scope for the imagination. **99**

Captions on page 330.

Haute Couture. Fall-Winter 1969-70.
Trouser suit with maxi overcoat
in double-face wool with python motif.
Photo Giampaolo Barbieri.

Page 202
Haute Couture. Fall-Winter 1987-88.
Detail of sequin embroidery
in tiger motif.
Photo Janos Grapow/
Archivio Valentino.

Page 203
Haute Couture. Fall-Winter 1967-68.
Tiger-motif wool coat and trousers
with black jersey tunic.
Photo Franco Rubartelli/
Archivio Valentino.

66 For me, white *is* color! White is one of the things that brings me luck. I remember the 1967 collection that I dedicated to Jackie Kennedy, for whom I designed 12 white dresses. It was a formidable success. I always like white because it stands for the lightness of summer, for purity. White can be used in such different ways. I can remember an old box of white lace that had been given to one of my aunts by Countess Asti; it was the purest joy. It was that box of lace that gave me the idea of painting the stockings of models with lace patterns — back in the sixties. At the time there were only plain stockings, so I started a new trend. White also stands for dreams. **99**

Page 205
Haute Couture Uomo. Fall-Winter 1968-69.
White-on-white embroidered vest.
Photo Ugo Mulas.

Page 207
Haute Couture. Spring-Summer 1969.
White dress and cape trimmed with large pleated flounce.

Pages 208-209
Haute Couture. Fall-Winter 1968-69.
White wool dress with large cape. Lace-up boots.
Photo Norman Parkinson/Courtesy *Vogue* © 1968 Edizioni Condé Nast S.p.A.

Haute Couture. Fall-Winter 1968-69.
Trouser suit with fox-fur trim.
Photo Regi Relang/Courtesy Verlag Hans
Schöner © *30 Jahre Mode Italien*.

Haute Couture. Fall-Winter 1965-66.
Coat in white double gabardine wool,
kimono-style sleeves.
Photo Franco Rubartelli/Archivio Valentino.

Haute Couture. Fall-Winter 1974-75.
Flowing reversible cape
with large pockets.
Photo Archivio Valentino.

Haute Couture. Spring-Summer 1970.
Straight, double-breasted coat,
with long stitched ribbing motifs
at the waist and the shoulders.
Photo Archivio Valentino.

Haute Couture. Spring-Summer 1970.
Double wool suit with short jacket accentuated
by stitched ribbing and short skirt.
Photo Barry Lategan/Courtesy *Vogue*
© 1970 Edizioni Condé Nast S.p.A.

Haute Couture. Spring-Summer 1968.
Coat with pockets decorated with the ''V''
motif in gold-colored metal.
Photo Archivio Valentino.

Haute Couture. Fall-Winter 1969-70.
Crepe evening dress with poncho trimmed
with ostrich feathers.
Photo Willy Rizzo/Archivio Valentino.

Page 212
Haute Couture. Fall-Winter 1971-72.
White astrakhan fur, trenchcoat cut.
Photo Archivio Valentino.

Haute Couture. Fall-Winter 1968-69.
White chiffon embroidered dress
with ostrich feather trim.
Photo Giampaolo Barbieri.

Page 215
Haute Couture. Spring-Summer 1968.
White cotton evening suits with pearls
and rhinestones embroidery.
Photo Henry Clarke/Courtesy
Vogue © 1968 Condé Nast
Publications Inc.

Haute Couture. Fall-Winter 1968-69.
White wool coat with cock's feather trim on edges and hem.
Photo Giampaolo Barbieri.

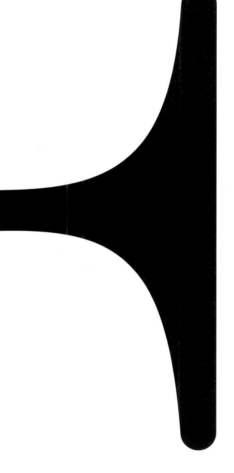

Folk

Spain
Russia
The Arabian Night
Central Europe
The Orient

66 Traveling always stimulates desires; or rather, the desire to travel moves me to depict the images that various countries may produce. The inspiration that the world offers me is unlimited, but over the years the way of expressing it has completely changed. I hate the period around 1970, because all fashion designers, including myself, were too close, too faithful to the themes that inspired us. Nowadays I know that I react like a painter: I am freer, more detached, vis-à-vis such influences. Nevertheless, all manner of things may attract me: Hungary, Bavaria in Ludwig's day, China, or some kitschy show I happened to see in a faraway land. But the result will not so closely resemble the thing that inspired it. **99**

Page 219
Collage.
Atelier Valentino.
Photo Janos Grapow.

Page 221
Haute Couture. Fall-Winter 1978-79.
Trouser suit with Chinese patterns.
Drawing Michael Meyring.

Pages 222-223
Haute Couture. Fall-Winter 1983-84.
Sequin-encrusted evening dress with black jet bead fringe.
Photo Gary Deane.

221

Page 225
Haute Couture. Fall-Winter 1983-84.
Fur accessories and rhinestone jewelry.
Photo Giampaolo Barbieri.

1 Haute Couture. Fall-Winter 1979-80. Red wool redingote
with brown velvet insets. Photo Regi Relang/Courtesy
Verlag Hans Schöner © *30 Jahre Mode Italien.*
2 Haute Couture - Uomo/Donna. Fall-Winter 1969-70. Donna:
ample cape and fur hat, ''Anna Karenina'' style, with fur trim.
Uomo: maxi overcoat with fur hat.
Photo Francesco Scavullo.

Haute Couture. Spring-Summer
1988.
Gem dress. Mini torero's bolero
and little dress in black silk crepe
with openwork rhinestone
embroidery.
Photo David Bailey/
Archivio Valentino.

Page 227
Haute Couture. Fall-Winter
1988-89.
Ruched, romantic, Spanish-style
blouse with lace insets.
Photo Alexandre
Weinberger/*WWD*.

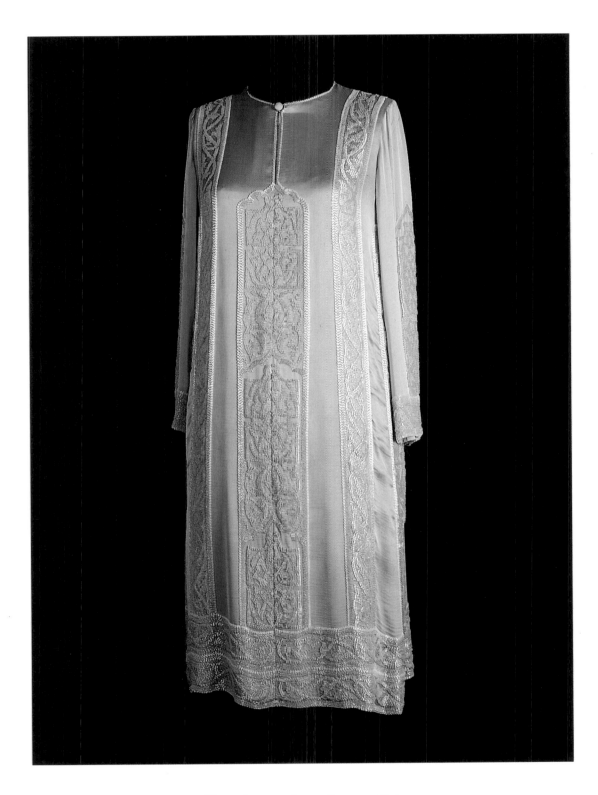

Haute Couture. Spring-Summer 1976.
Embroidered tunic with motifs taken from mosque mosaics.
Photo Janos Grapow/Archivio Valentino.

Page 228
Prêt-à-porter. Fall-Winter 1983-84.
Brown lamé evening gown inspired by oriental painting.
Photo Barry Lategan/Courtesy *Vogue* © 1983 Condé Nast Verlag GmbH.

Prêt-à-porter. Fall-Winter 1977-78.
Group photo with clothing inspired by Ludwig of Bavaria.
Photo Deborah Turbeville/Archivio Valentino.

Page 230
Prêt-à-porter. Fall-Winter 1980-81.
Dress with large shawl of Tyrolean inspiration.
Photo Barry Lategan/Courtesy *Vogue* © 1980 Edizioni Condé Nast S.p.A.

Arab-inspired harem trousers
with African-style accessories.
Left, belt with
African-inspired buckle.
Photos Nicolas Bruant/
Archivio Valentino.

Haute Couture. Fall-Winter 1965-66.
Palazzo pajama: fabrics with Indian
and Indonesian motifs, coral
and gemstone accessories.
Photo Elsa Haerter/
Grazia © Mondadori Press.

Prêt-à-porter. Fall-Winter 1970-71.
Maxidress with fabric inspired
by Turkish folk motifs.
Photo Irving Penn/Courtesy *Vogue*
© 1970 Condé Nast
Publications Inc.

Page 236
Prêt-à-porter. Fall-Winter 1970-71.
Hooded dress: fabric with Persian motifs.
Photo Courtesy *Harper's Bazaar Italia*.

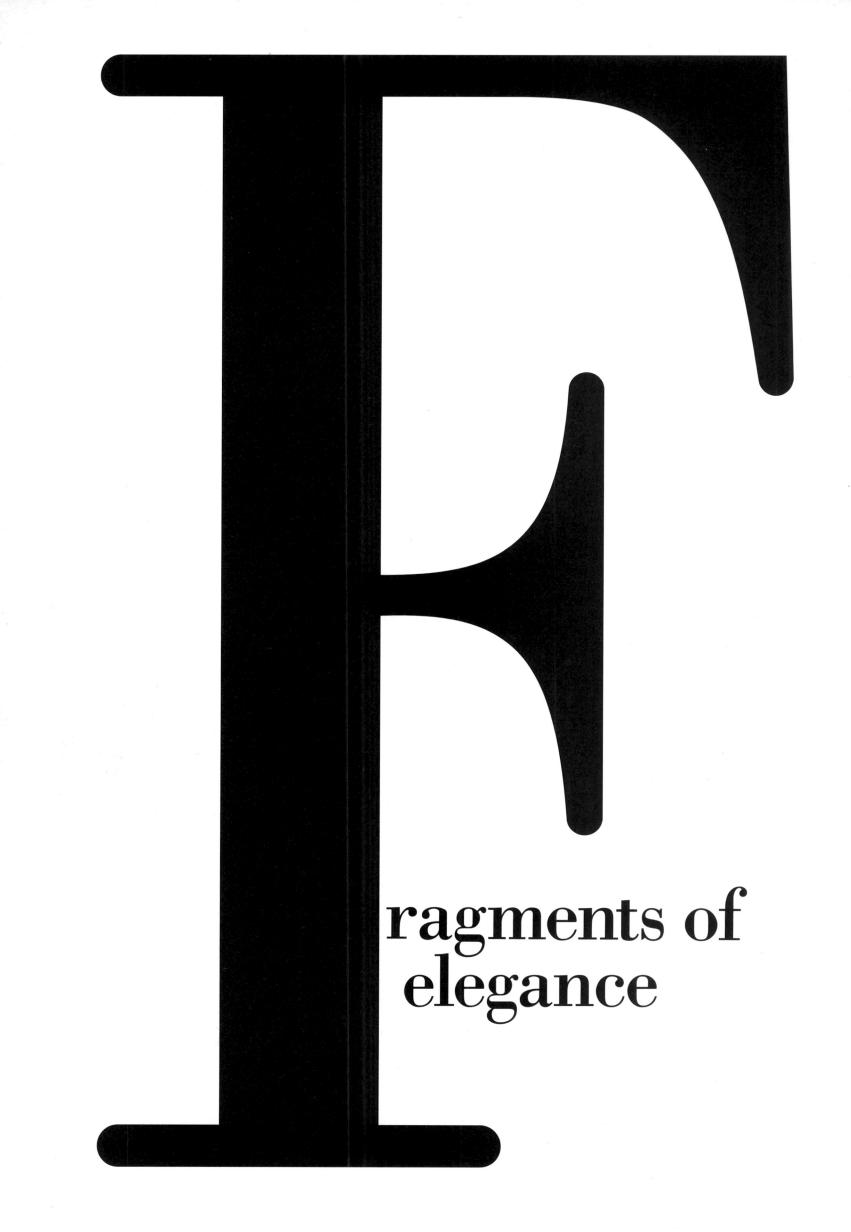

Fragments of
elegance

66 Just as I can get enthusiastic about one of those evening birds that I like so much, I can completely fall for a woman who's dressed quite simply, but has the audacity to draw attention to herself with some small detail, thus becoming so remarkable that the way she's dressed no longer matters. Some out-of-this world detail invented by a woman will

make her more important to me than one dressed up in all the colors of the rainbow, who just looks ordinary. For instance, a woman wearing a sweater who has the nerve to pin on it a handkerchief covered with sequins or colored stones can make my day. I like women who realize that something quite small can become everything. **99**

Haute Couture. Spring-Summer 1988.
Medieval-inspired jewelry.
Photo Marco Lanza/*Moda In*,
n. 4, 1988, Zanfi Editori.

Page 243
Haute Couture. Fall-Winter 1985-86.
Crystal jewelry.
Photo Susan Lamér/*Frankfurter
Allgemeine Magazin.*

Haute Couture. Fall-Winter 1982-83.
Black satin and gold leather shoes.
Photo Renato Grignaschi/
Courtesy *Vogue* © 1982 Edizioni
Condé Nast S.p.A.

Page 244
Beauty-Bags 1989.
Clutch bag embossed with paisley pattern.
Photo Walter Chin/Archivio Valentino.

Prêt-à-porter.
Spring-Summer 1972.
Belt with large rose.
Photo Frank Horvat/Courtesy
Vogue © 1972 Condé
Nast Publications Inc.

Page 246
Prêt-à-porter. Fall-Winter
1988-89.
Evening shoes with exquisite
golden embroidery.
Photo Fabrizio Ferri/*Donna*.

Haute Couture. Fall-Winter 1971-72.
An Egyptian-inspired ebony and diamond
snake brooch.
Photo Oliviero Toscani.

Page 248
Haute Couture. Fall-Winter 1988-89.
A cascade of jewelry with chromatic interplay of different
types of stones, pearls, and metals.
Photo Tyen/Archivio Valentino.

Pages 250-251
Haute Couture. Fall-Winter 1983-84.
African-style bracelet.
Photo Bill Silano/Courtesy *Vogue* © 1983
Edizioni Condé Nast S.p.A.

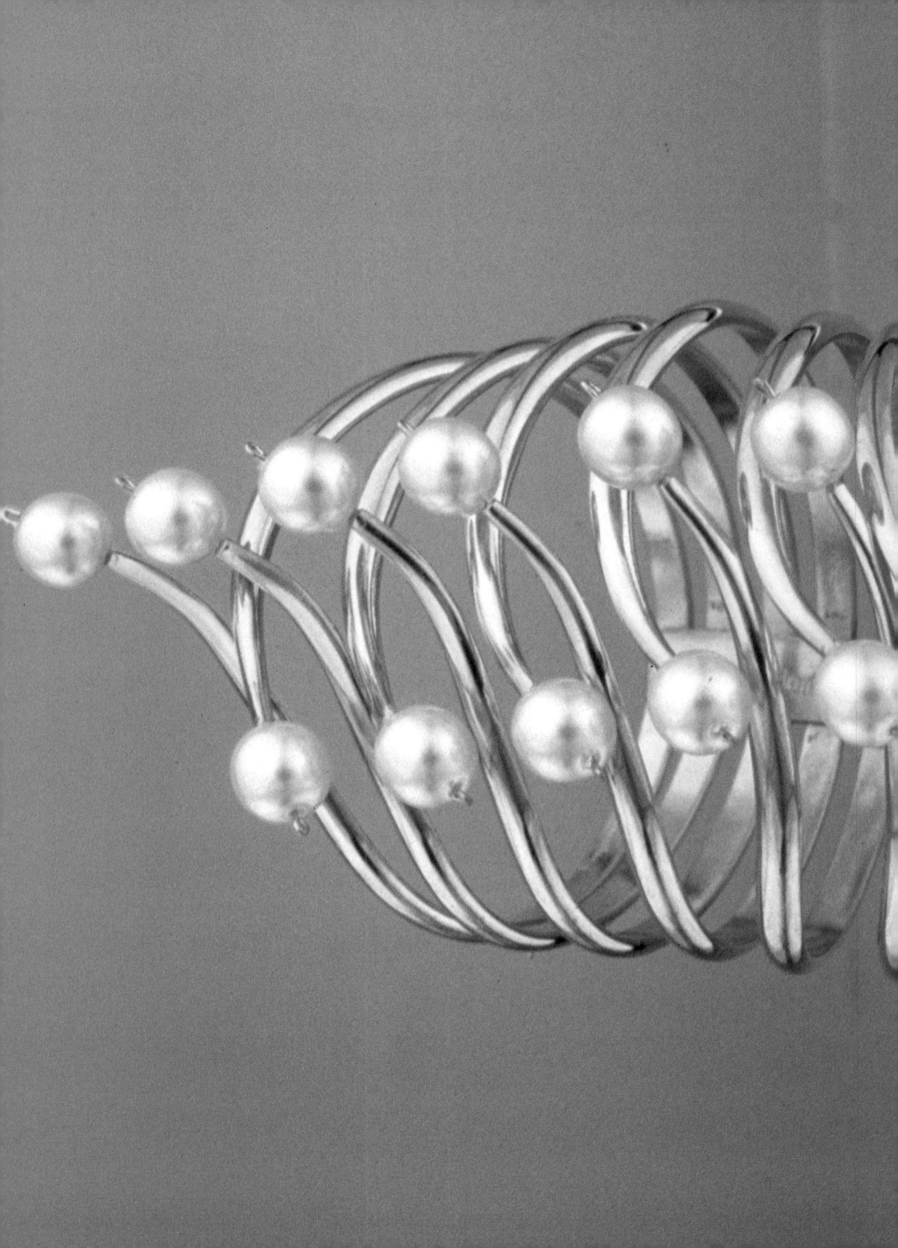

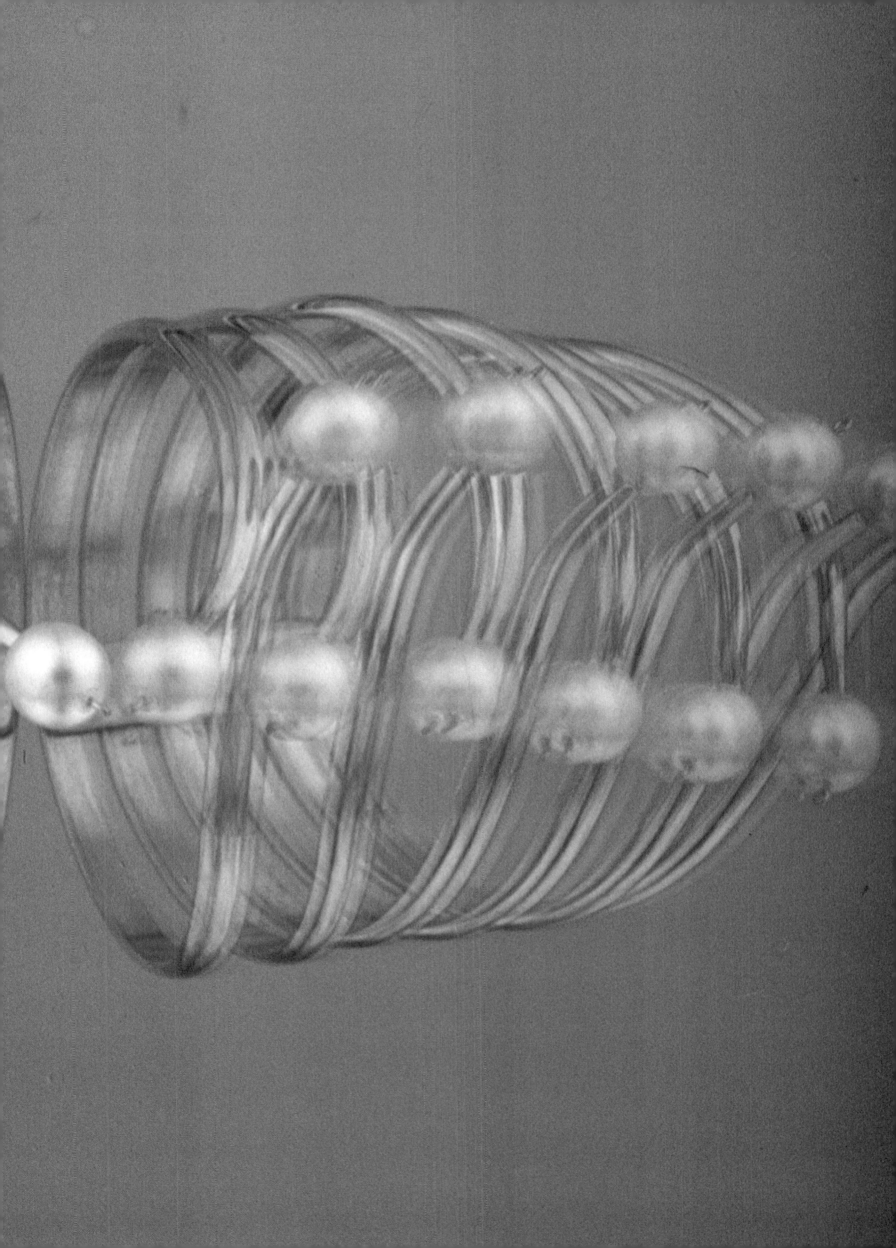

1 Haute Couture. Spring-Summer 1963. Military style feather hat. Photo Archivio Valentino.   2 Haute Couture. Fall-Winter 1989-90. Multi-tiered pearl necklace. Photo Serge Barbeau/*L'Officiel*. 3 Haute Couture. Fall-Winter 1988-89. Brimmed hat with ruched ribbon band. Photo Daniel Povda.   4 Haute Couture. Fall-Winter 1968-69. Griffin buckle. Photo Giampaolo Barbieri.   5 Haute Couture. Spring-Summer 1987. Rhinestone and gemstone drop earrings. Photo David Bailey.   6 Prêt-à-porter. Spring-Summer 1986. Rhinestone-encrusted sixties-style foulard. Photo Sergio Caminata/*Donna*. 7 Haute Couture. Spring-Summer 1985. Crocodile clutch bag with spiral closure. Photo Jim Reiher.   8 Haute Couture. Fall-Winter 1985-86. Cockney-style beret, decorated with pearls. 9 Haute Couture. Fall-Winter 1989-90. Exquisite raised embroidery with diamonds and colored feathers and gemstones, of baroque inspiration. Photo Serge Barbeau/*L'Officiel*.   10 Prêt-à-porter. Spring-Summer 1983. Sandals for evening wear with spiral ankle strap. Photo Alberta Tiburzi.   11 Haute Couture. Fall-Winter 1969-70. Art nouveau snake belt. Photo David Bailey/Archivio Valentino.

Page 252
Haute Couture. Fall-Winter 1987-88. Embroidered tights and black satin jeweled sandal. Photo Giovanni Gastel/*Donna*.

Page 253
Haute Couture. Fall-Winter 1988-89. Bracelet with small diamond-encrusted spheres. Photo Courtesy *Donna*.

Page 255
Haute Couture. Fall-Winter 1987-88. Red satin embroidered shoes. Photo Albert Watson/ Courtesy *Vogue*
© 1987 Edizioni Condé Nast S.p.A.

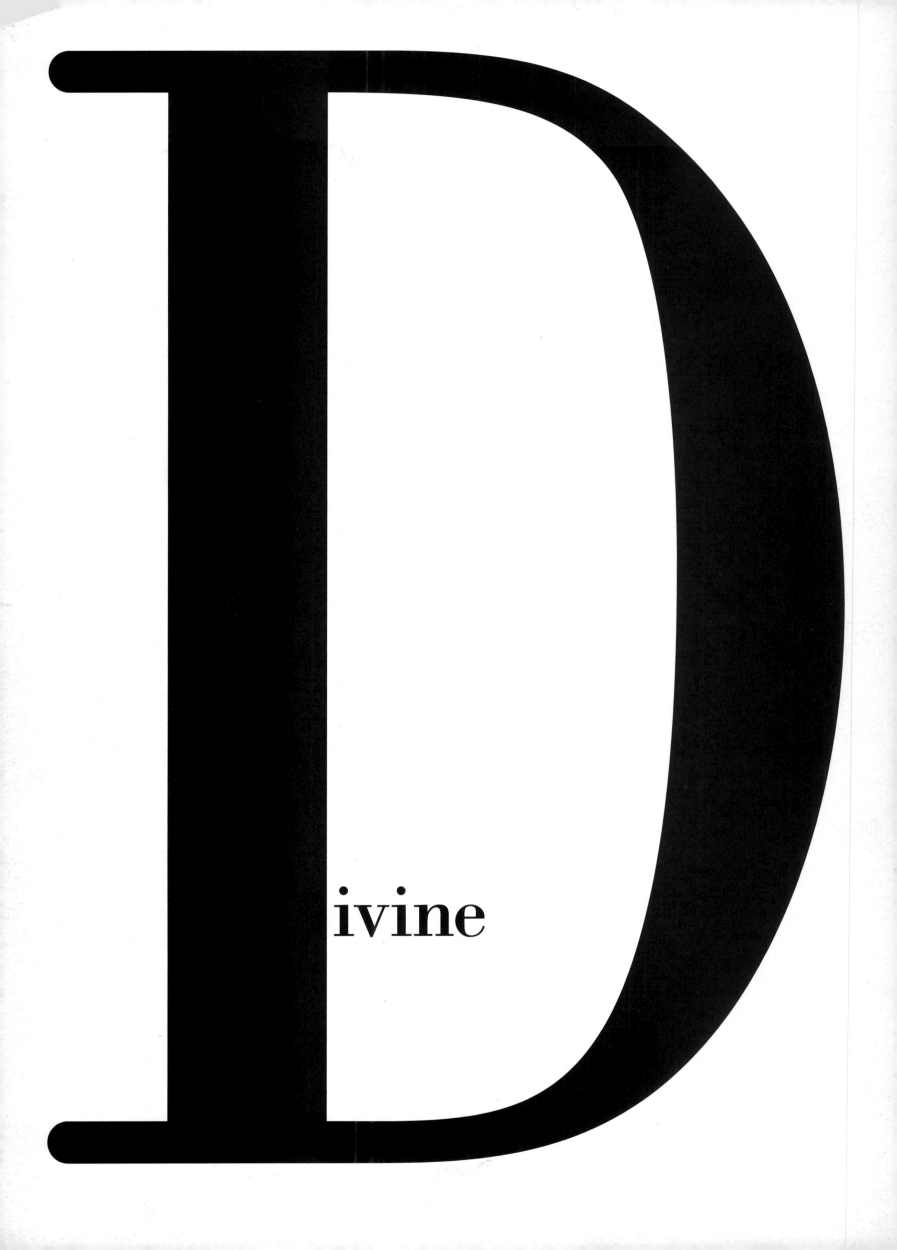

Divine

66La Divine is a dream woman. When I was young, I used to be enthralled by the great stars of the screen. That was the beginning of my boundless admiration for women of symbolic greatness such as Lana Turner, Rita Hayworth, Ava Gardner, and Marlene Dietrich. Above all, Marlene in *Seven Sinners* and Greta Garbo in *Queen Christina*. Those were the days when the masses fed on such stupendous images, feasting their eyes upon women who were sublime but beyond their reach and who inhabited a world that was somehow exalted and unreal. And so I've always cherished within me images of these untouchable women, clothed in fabulous dresses, and in pursuit of my dream I have continued to create dresses for them: my 'divines.' **99**

Page 257
Prêt-à-porter. Fall-Winter 1984-85.
Black velvet sheath-dress.
Photo Toni Thorimbert.

Page 259
Haute Couture. Fall-Winter 1965-66.
Princess Luciana Pignatelli wearing a richly embroidered ostrich feather cape.
Photo Archivio Valentino.

Haute Couture. Fall-Winter 1990-91.
Christy Turlington wearing an
embroidered crystal motif suit.
Photo Patrick Demarchelier/Courtesy
Vogue © 1990 Edizioni
Condé Nast S.p.A.

Prêt-à-porter. Fall-Winter 1987-88.
Paulina Porizkova.
Photo Arthur Elgort/Courtesy *Vogue* © 1987
Condé Nast Publications Inc.

Haute Couture. Fall-Winter 1988-89.
Diane de Witt.
Photo Arthur Elgort/Courtesy *Vogue* © 1988
Edizioni Condé Nast S.p.A.

Page 263
Haute Couture. Fall-Winter 1990-91.
Christy Turlington.
Photo Patrick Demarchelier/Courtesy *Vogue* © 1990
Edizioni Condé Nast S.p.A.

Prêt-à-porter. Fall-Winter 1977-78.
Models wearing evening gowns in Ludwig of Bavaria style.
Photo Deborah Turbeville.

Haute Couture. Fall-Winter 1989-90.
Form-fitting evening gown with lattice back ending in a bow.
Photo Sante D'Orazio.

Haute Couture. Fall-Winter 1965-66.
Veruschka wearing a red crepe dress and a feather cape.
Photo Henry Clarke/Courtesy *Vogue* © 1965 Condé Nast Publications Inc.

1952. Wedding gown in white lace designed by Valentino
for the Wanda sisters' wedding.
Photo Gary Deane.

Captions on page 330.

Prêt-à-porter. Fall-Winter 1989-90. Paris. Black satin ball gown with bow. Photo Henry Clarke/Courtesy *Vogue*

Captions on page 330.

...outure. Spring-Summer 1989.
...spired by the *Nike* of Samothraces,
...draped evening gown with embroidered
insets of garlands of small
silver leaves and flowers.
Rome, Accademia Valentino.
Photo Daniel Jouanneau.

Haute Couture. Fall-Winter 1986-87.
Red silk crepe dress in neoclassical style
Photo Noelle Hoeppe

Haute Couture. Fall-Winter 1961-62.
White evening gown with train, edged in precious stones.
Photo Archivio Valentino.

Haute Couture. Fall-Winter 1978-79.
Pleated pink lamé evening gown enriched
by ruches.
Photo Archivio Valentino.

Haute Couture. Spring-Summer 1972.
Flowing evening gown with lace inset.
Photo Archivio Valentino.

Haute Couture. Fall-Winter 1974-75.
Salmon pink chiffon evening dress
with finely ruched bodice and three
flounces edged in marabou feathers.
Photo Archivio Valentino.

Page 276
Haute Couture. Spring-Summer 1965.
Red crepe evening dress with full
embroidered ostrich cape.
Photo Archivio Valentino.

Prêt-à-porter. Fall-Winter 1988-89.
Evening gown with flounced lace
and tulle skirt.
Photo Stefano Massimo/*Grazia*
© Mondadori Press.

Page 278
Prêt-à-porter. Fall-Winter 1988-89.
Evening dress made up of a violet
bodice on a yellow-gold skirt with
exquisite openwork embroidery.
Photo David Seidner.

Page 280
Haute Couture. Fall-Winter 1990-91.
Brocade suit with velvet
insets; chiffon blouse and velvet skirt
with sequin embroidery.
Photo Patrick Demarchelier/
Courtesy *Vogue* © 1990 Edizioni
Condé Nast S.p.A.

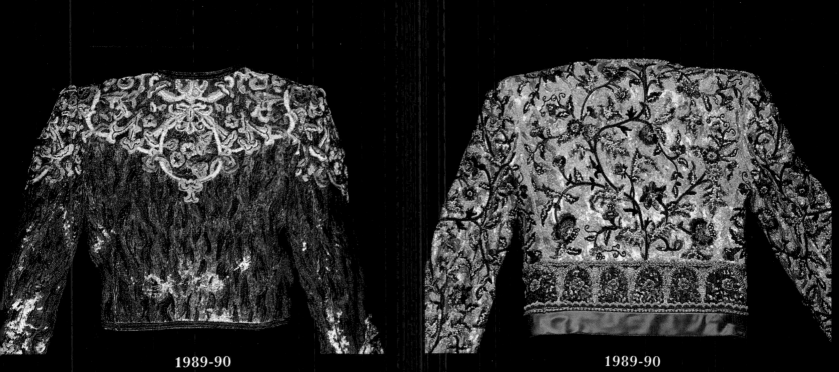

1989-90

1989-90

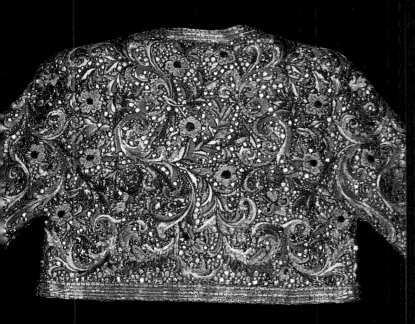

1988-89

1989

1988-89

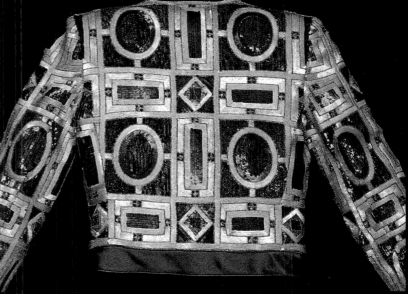

1989-90

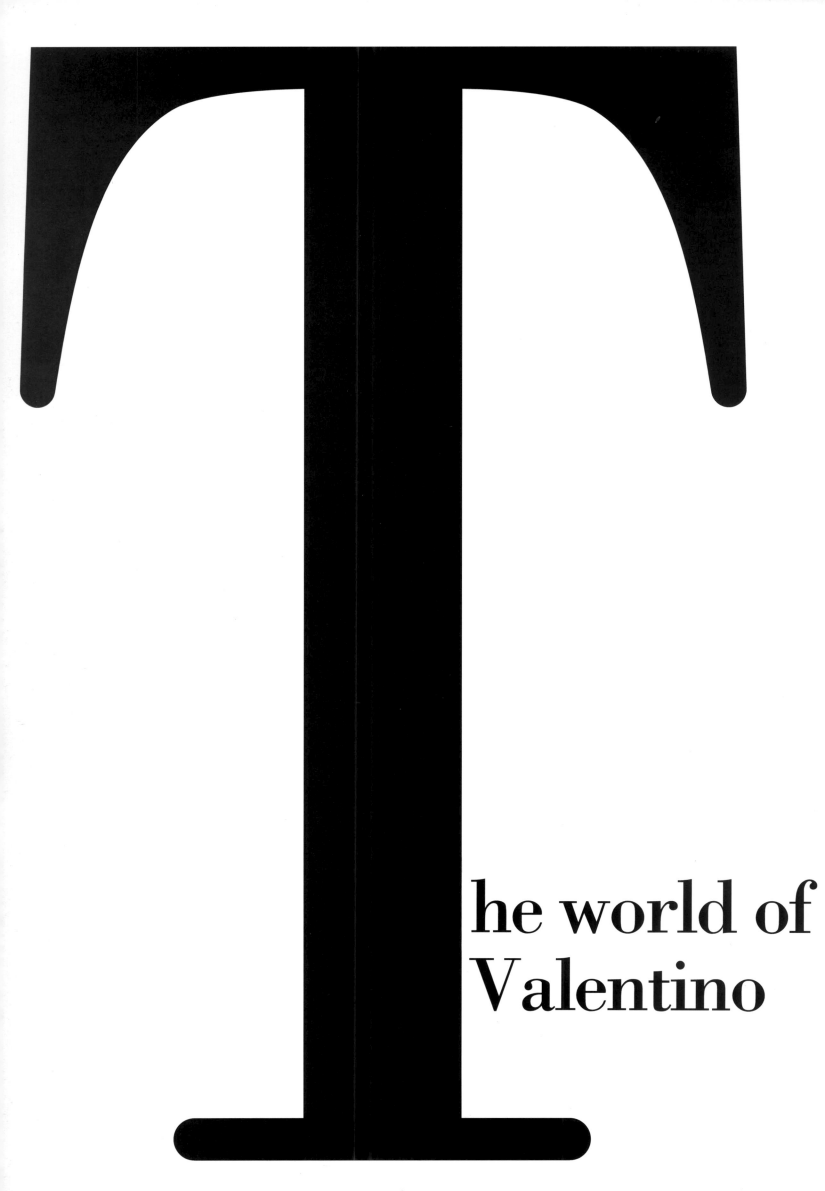

The world of
Valentino

66My private world is a simple world. Every day I thank heaven for the life that it has given me. I have a great appetite for splendor, but at the same time very simple tastes. Nothing for me is better than a plate of thin pasta, *pennette* with tomato and basil sauce. I could eat it morning, noon, and night, at teatime, lunch, and dinner; it is so satisfying. But also, nothing is more seductive for me than the sight of those sublime gardens in Italy. I will always remember a crumbling wall under a great cascade of white roses that I saw at Marella Agnelli's home; I cherish my memories of the most incredible landscapes in Italy. When I am on a glacier, deep inside of me I am filled with emotion: before these marvelous immensities, everything, trivialities, feelings take on their true perspective. And the man I am at that moment knows. **99**

Page 283
Photo of the set for Luchino Visconti's film *The Leopard*.
Photo Giambattista Poletto/Courtesy Titanus.

Page 285
Photo Galen Rowell/Peter Arnold Inc./Grazia Neri.

Valentino may love fashion and its fabrics, homes and their furnishings, but one thing is clear: above all, Valentino loves life. Whether he is planning a trip, entertaining his friends, hiring a cook (only the best will do), or hunting down the most incredible finds in every major metropolis, the great couturier is caught up in it all with the same enthusiasm, the same relish. He is thankful for all that life has to offer him. ''When I am alone, which upon occasion does happen,'' says Valentino ''my greatest joy is to go settle into my favorite corner for reading or for sketching.'' The idea could not have been expressed more simply. But when it comes to guessing which room of his many homes Valentino prefers, he is hesitant about favoring this or that element, this or that object. Rome is his headquarters. But, paradoxically, since he works so intensely, he has little opportunity to enjoy the handsome neoclassical villa in via Appia. Capri is his summer vacation spot where life is simple. In Gstaad he owns a chalet that lends itself to long winter evenings. In London he recreated the elegantly languid atmosphere of the Victorian gentry; while in New York where he spends about one

A few interior and exterior views of Valentino's home in Rome.
Photos 1, 3, 5, Fritz von der Schulenburg. Photo 2, David Lees/*People*/Grazia Neri. Photo 4, Karen Radkai/Archivio Valentino. Photo 6, François Halard/Visual Team.

Interior view of Valentino's home in Rome, with painting by Fernando Botero.
Photo Fritz von der Schulenburg.

month of the year, Valentino owns an apartment, very urbane, with heavy red velvet draperies. But it is perhaps on his boat where he is able to forget the responsibilities linked to his ever-growing business. "The sea is the ultimate in protection. I leave everything behind me!"

When Valentino was just starting out in Paris, he lived in two *chambres de bonne*. He bought furniture by Boulle for a song at the *Marché aux Puces*, added some curtains and a few couches in *toile de Jouy*. It was not much, but it was charming. Success brought with it his first purchases: a seventeenth-century polychrome commode made in Rome, then an

Rome, Palazzo Mignanelli. The office of Giancarlo Giammetti, president and managing director of the Valentino group. Photo François Hallard/Visual Team.

eighteenth-century *encoignure* and two still lifes that the *couturier* still has. The collecting mania has taken hold of him, and it will never let him go. Wherever he is, on the eve of a fashion show or between two fittings, the man (who is always pressed for time) slips away at the end to go in pursuit of the rare object, the handsome piece of furniture.

Despite the diversity and the abundance of his homes, his interiors could not be less formal, less affected; they are a continual source of delight to the eye. "When I conceive an interior the first thing I think about is how many people I will be able to seat.

Discomfort along with pretention are the two worst things that can happen to a home.''

Valentino has a passion for the most beautiful homes and the objects to fill them. It would therefore be unfair not to point out the sympathetic chord that this lively interest strikes in his partner, Giancarlo Giammetti. In both of their homes, as in their respective activities, their aesthetic is complementary: the atmosphere that surrounds the *couturier* evokes the Proustian charm of *temps perdus* from *The Leopard* of Lampedusa to Oscar Wilde's Belgravia. The businessman's setting is more contemporary: geared for action, it takes its inspiration from the Viennese Secession, the thirties, modern art. But they have

Rome, Palazzo Mignanelli. Valentino's office. Photo François Halard/Visual Team.

the same unbridled passion for luxury and the same generosity. It is this curiosity that makes them alert to the slightest creative glimmer from wherever it comes.

Though Valentino loves to see his surroundings evolve and leads a cosmopolitan life, he would view it badly to constantly renew his interiors: ''A clear personality flaw.'' In all the senses of the term, he is creative. He wants his homes to conserve their integrity, to mature, to acquire a patina and slowly evolve.

It is the *couturier's* business to have this wisdom: ''When I was a young designer, I made

collections that incorporated two hundred thousand ideas where just thirty would have been enough. With time I learned to make real clothing for real women whose needs are real too. With homes it is the same thing. One must bear in mind certain constants that can be repeated in any period. There are certain traditions, proportions, and colors that must be respected. For me, for example, fabrics are a very important point of departure, the best way to personalize an interior. Along with very beautiful objects. The object has a magical effect on me. Later, one must learn to eliminate. Little by little one learns to distinguish that subtle line between too much and not enough that is called equilibrium. In fashion or in decor, it is the same thing: simplicity must never be redolent of poverty. One may even overdo, but only if it is done with great flair. To know how to exaggerate in moderation will always be the most difficult thing.''

François Baudot

London, a few views of the interior
of Valentino's home.
Photos Fritz von der Schulenburg.

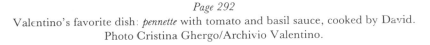

Page 292
Valentino's favorite dish: *pennette* with tomato and basil sauce, cooked by David.
Photo Cristina Ghergo/Archivio Valentino.

Page 293
View of the Tuscan countryside.
Photo Marella Agnelli.

In our time fashion has definitely vanquished religion as the opiate of the masses. But Valentino's work is an exception. Although he has made his pact with the world as it is — with his licensed products, ready-to-wear, and so forth — his sensibility belongs to the happy few.

I use that expression with an accent on "happy." A Valentino collection at its best is an explosion of joy, a celebration not just of the glitter of wealth but of the sensual delights of life at the top. Of pleasure — like the joy of two lovers who hop into bed believing they own the world — ah yes, there's a lot of healthy sexiness in Valentino's style.

We all know that in real life rich people are not always happy and that Valentino himself may not be short of hang-ups despite his success, but here's another important thing you have to recognize in his work: Valentino is a straightforward idealist.

This ideal, this Gatsby-like fascination with rarified, elegant bonheur may have its moral detractors. I happen to think a little of it is necessary to civilization, and I'm happy that in the case of Valentino it's in good hands. I used the word *straightforward*. I mean he doesn't deform his ideal because he's ashamed in our times to come right out with it. His fashion isn't ironic, it isn't off the wall, it isn't a cerebral diversion or worst of all, a publicity farce in the form of a tiresome intellectual joke. He doesn't make "avant-garde statements" to impress the multitudes.

Sometimes Valentino gets carried away with his enthusiasm and we get excess. But it's always innocent excess with a note of joy.

The distinctions between art and commerce or art and applied art have been blurred in our time. Without judging this historical change, I'd like to make reference to art in defining Valentino's work. You could say he is conceptually naïve and technically a master. Naive in the sense that his beliefs are untempered infatuations. He intends only one level of meaning. A master? You can count on your fingers the people in this world who have his technique. *Couturier* is a much-abused word nowadays, but this man is a true *couturier*.

I happened to have been in Valentino's couture house in Rome when the smell wafting up from a McDonald's below was driving him crazy. It wasn't just a smell to him, it was a violation. All the same, I don't think Valentino — though he is known to eat off vermeil tableware — is really that much of a snob. As with Balenciaga, his style has a note of well-targeted emulation — the fascination of a talented person born poor but with an affinity for the taste of the most refined. His style does not arise from the self-adulation of a rock star. He hasn't learned elegance at a remove, from magazines and the latest movies. His clients have refined him. However, that kind of inspiring clientele is getting harder and harder to find.

Nonetheless, Valentino moves ahead with his times. I don't know for sure, but I'd guess he has even eaten a little fast food here or there. He just wouldn't let fast food stink up his life where he truly lives. He won his case against McDonald's, and he wins his case on the runways season after season, because after all is said, his creations are beautiful things. And a work of beauty stands firm as a work of beauty, no matter what is blowing on the wind.

Gerry Dryansky

1960
1990

*Alta Moda
Primavera-Estate*

*Alta Moda
Autunno-Inverno*

*Alta Moda
Primavera-Estate*

*Alta Moda
Autunno-Inverno*

Disegni originali di Valentino

1961

Alta Moda
Primavera-Estate

Alta Moda
Autunno-Inverno

1962

Alta Moda
Primavera-Estate

Alta Moda
Autunno-Inverno

Disegni originali di Valentino

1963

1964

*Alta Moda
Primavera-Estate*

*Alta Moda
Autunno-Inverno*

*Alta Moda
Primavera-Estate*

*Alta Moda
Autunno-Inverno*

Disegni originali di Valentino

1965

1966

*Alta Moda
Primavera-Estate*

*Alta Moda
Autunno-Inverno*

*Alta Moda
Primavera-Estate*

*Alta Moda
Autunno-Inverno*

Disegni originali di Valentino

*Alta Moda
Primavera-Estate*

*Alta Moda
Autunno-Inverno*

*Pret-à-porter
Autunno-Inverno*

Disegni originali di Valentino

*Alta Moda
Primavera-Estate*

*Alta Moda
Autunno-Inverno*

*Pret-à-porter
Autunno-Inverno*

*Alta Moda
Primavera-Estate*

*Alta Moda
Autunno-Inverno*

*Pret-à-porter
Primavera-Estate*

Disegni originali di Valentino

*Alta Moda
Primavera-Estate*

*Alta Moda
Autunno-Inverno*

*Pret-à-porter
Primavera-Estate*

Alta Moda
Primavera-Estate

Alta Moda
Autunno-Inverno

1976

Alta Moda
Primavera-Estate

Alta Moda
Autunno-Inverno

Pret-à-porter
Autunno-Inverno

*Alta Moda
Primavera-Estate*

*Alta Moda
Autunno-Inverno*

*Pret-à-porter
Primavera-Estate*

*Pret-à-porter
Autunno-Inverno*

*Alta Moda
Primavera-Estate*

*Alta Moda
Autunno-Inverno*

*Pret-à-porter
Primavera-Estate*

*Pret-à-porter
Autunno-Inverno*

*Alta Moda
Primavera-Estate*

*Alta Moda
Autunno-Inverno*

*Pret-à-porter
Primavera-Estate*

*Pret-à-porter
Autunno-Inverno*

*Alta Moda
Primavera-Estate*

*Alta Moda
Autunno-Inverno*

*Pret-à-porter
Primavera-Estate*

*Pret-à-porter
Autunno-Inverno*

*Alta Moda
Primavera-Estate*

*Alta Moda
Autunno-Inverno*

*Pret-à-porter
Primavera-Estate*

*Pret-à-porter
Autunno-Inverno*

1981

Alta Moda
Primavera-Estate

Alta Moda
Autunno-Inverno

Pret-à-porter
Primavera-Estate

Pret-à-porter
Autunno-Inverno

1982

*Alta Moda
Primavera-Estate*

*Alta Moda
Autunno-Inverno*

*Pret-à-porter
Primavera-Estate*

*Pret-à-porter
Autunno-Inverno*

*Alta Moda
Primavera-Estate*

*Alta Moda
Autunno-Inverno*

*Pret-à-porter
Primavera-Estate*

*Pret-à-porter
Autunno-Inverno*

*Alta Moda
Primavera-Estate*

*Alta Moda
Autunno-Inverno*

*Pret-à-porter
Primavera-Estate*

*Pret-à-porter
Autunno-Inverno*

*Alta Moda
Primavera-Estate*

*Alta Moda
Autunno-Inverno*

*Pret-à-porter
Primavera-Estate*

*Pret-à-porter
Autunno-Inverno*

*Alta Moda
Primavera-Estate*

*Alta Moda
Autunno-Inverno*

*Pret-à-porter
Primavera-Estate*

*Pret-à-porter
Autunno-Inverno*

1986

Alta Moda
Primavera-Estate

Alta Moda
Autunno-Inverno

Pret-à-porter
Primavera-Estate

Pret-à-porter
Autunno-Inverno

*Alta Moda
Primavera-Estate*

*Alta Moda
Autunno-Inverno*

*Pret-à-porter
Primavera-Estate*

*Pret-à-porter
Autunno-Inverno*

*Alta Moda
Primavera-Estate*

*Alta Moda
Autunno-Inverno*

*Pret-à-porter
Primavera-Estate*

*Pret-à-porter
Autunno-Inverno*

*Alta Moda
Primavera-Estate*

*Alta Moda
Autunno-Inverno*

*Pret-à-porter
Primavera-Estate*

*Pret-à-porter
Autunno-Inverno*

Alta Moda
Primavera-Estate

Alta Moda
Autunno-Inverno

Pret-à-porter
Primavera-Estate

Pret-à-porter
Autunno-Inverno

*Alta Moda
Primavera-Estate*

*Pret-à-porter
Primavera-Estate*

*Alta Moda
Autunno-Inverno*

*Pret-à-porter
Autunno-Inverno*

Prêt-à-porter. Primavera-Estate 1991.

Atelier sketches
selected from the over
20,000 drawings
of the Maison Valentino.

1960
―――
1990

Page 67

1 Prêt-à-porter. Fall-Winter 1987-88. Red satin evening gown. Photo Steven Meisel/Archivio Valentino. 2 Haute Couture. Fall-Winter 1988-89. Red chiffon evening gown with overlapping pleated flounces. Photo Archivio Valentino. 3 Haute Couture. Fall-Winter 1984-85. Red crepe evening dress with long V-neckline in back and diamond clasps. Photo J. Noël L'Harmeroult/*Amica*. 4 Haute Couture. Fall-Winter 1967-68. Red wool brocade suit with tortoise-shell buttons and snakeskin belt with gold V-shaped buckle, fur hat. Photo Archivio Valentino. 5 Haute Couture. Fall-Winter 1989-90. Black velvet evening dress with red satin cape. Photo Sante D'Orazio/Courtesy *Vogue* © 1989 Les Publications Condé Nast S.A. 6 Prêt-à-porter. Fall-Winter 1983-84 Roomy cartwheel mantle in red wool. Photo Fabrizio Ferri/*Donna*. 7 Haute Couture. Fall-Winter 1987-88. Redingote in red wool with high border of brown sable. Photo Arthur Elgort. 8 Haute Couture. Spring-Summer 1988. Red crepe and chiffon evening dress, with interlaced, knotted drapery. Photo David Bailey/Archivio Valentino. 9 Prêt-à-porter. Fall-Winter 1989-90. Red double wool redingote. Photo Eddy Kohli/*Marie-Claire* © Mondadori Press.

Page 91

1 Haute Couture. Fall-Winter 1963-64. Suit in double wool with dropped sleeves and showy buttons. 2 Haute Couture. Fall-Winter 1966-67. Space-age look short tunic in white double wool with long tight trousers and little helmet to match. 3 Haute Couture. Fall-Winter 1962-63. Empire line. Elegant flared overcoat in black wool with high waist, and two buttons and a flat bow at the stand-away collar band; jaguar fur hat. 4 Haute Couture. Fall-Winter 1962-63. Navy blue and mustard dress and overcoat in double wool with contrasting color inserts; crocodile hat. 5 Haute Couture. Fall-Winter 1966-67. Geometric-line suit in op art fabric. Photo Regi Relang/Courtesy Verlag Hans Schöner © *30 Jahre Mode Italien*. 6 Haute Couture. Fall-Winter 1965-66. Black and white printed silk minidress with pleated culottes and blouse; wool overcoat with the same print. 7 Haute Couture. Fall-Winter 1970-71. Dress with short jacket with colored sequins inspired by patchwork quilts. Photo Chris von Wangenheim/Archivio Valentino. 8 Haute Winter 1959-60. Gray redingote with straight skirt, collar and cuffs in brown velvet and otterskin hat. 9 Haute Couture. Spring-Summer 1970. Maxicoat with fine vertical tucked ribbing and miniskirt. Photo Regi Relang/Courtesy Verlag Hans Schöner © *30 Jahre Mode Italien*. 10 Haute Couture. Fall-Winter 1965-66. Double-breasted empire-line coat with black-and-white op art motifs. Photo Archivio Valentino. 11 Haute Couture. Fall-Winter 1962-63. Red wool coat with cockades as buttons. 12 Haute Couture. Spring-Summer 1969. Beige cloak and vest, white jumpsuit with large patch pockets and gold metal trimming. Photo Archivio Valentino. 13 Haute Couture. Fall-Winter 1965-66. Classic gray suit with wrap skirt; mink hat. 14 Haute Couture. Fall-Winter 1970-71. Hooded beige and brown lynx-trimmed suit. Photo Regi Relang/Courtesy Verlag Hans Schöner © *30 Jahre Mode Italien*. 15 Haute Couture. Fall-Winter 1963-64. Black-and-white suit in ponyskin with fur trim. Photo Archivio Valentino.

Page 92

1 Haute Couture. Fall-Winter 1965-66. Empire-line redingote in raised brocade with small half-belt. 2 Haute Couture. Fall-Winter 1960-67. Gold lace and brocade amphora-shaped cocktail dress. 3 Haute Couture. Fall-Winter 1962-63. Black satin evening gown with large bow at the waist and short bolero in gold lace. 4 Haute Couture. Fall-Winter 1963-64. Heavy pink satin evening gown with short jacket edged in organdy petals. Photo Leombruno Bodi/Archivio Valentino. 5 Haute Couture. Fall-Winter 1963-64. Empireline evening gown in heavy pink satin with roomy sleeves. 6 Haute Couture. Spring-Summer 1968. White collection. Gold lamé evening dress relief embroidered in small flower motif; skirt and scarf in silk chiffon; chainlink and wood belt. 7 Haute Couture. Fall-Winter 1974-75. Folksy palazzo pajama with long-fringed poncho; gold chain and coral belt. Photo Giampaolo Barbieri. 8 Haute Couture. Fall-Winter 1963-64. Palazzo pajama in white brocade fabric with belt and bow. 9 Haute Couture. Spring-Summer 1964. Little white organdy jacket with flounced edging over plain black tube dress. Photo Regi Relang/Courtesy Verlag Hans Schöner © *30 Jahre Mode Italien*. 10 Haute Couture. Spring-Summer 1967. Veruschka. Palazzo pajama in cotton satin with large panthers printed in black on a green ground. Photo Franco Rubartelli. 11 Haute Couture. Fall-Winter 1968-69. White silk evening gown. 12 Haute Couture. Fall-Winter 1961-62. Two-piece evening dress with jet-and gemstone-trimmed tunic. 13 Haute Couture. Fall-Winter 1968-69. Polka-dot palazzo pajama in white organdy with giant daisy edging. Photo David Bailey/Courtesy *Vogue* © 1968 Edizioni Condé Nast S.p.A. 14 Haute Couture. Spring-Summer 1959. Evening dress with petticoated white satin skirt and black chiffon blouse, decorated with two large white roses. Photo Archivio Valentino. 15 Haute Couture. Fall-Winter 1963-64. Low-waisted pink satin cocktail dress with amphora-shaped skirt; ruched neckline with tulle rose. Photo Archivio Valentino. 16 Haute Couture. Fall-Winter 1959-60. White satin cocktail

dress printed with floral motifs inspired by bougainvillea. Photo Archivio Valentino.

Page 130

1 Prêt-à-porter. Fall-Winter 1989-90. Black velvet evening dress with white draping. Photo Walter Chin/Archivio Valentino. 2 Haute Couture. Fall-Winter 1965-66. Black-and-white coat with op art motifs. Photo Archivio Valentino. 3 Haute Couture. Spring-Summer 1966. Dress with black-and-white op art motif. Photo Archivio Valentino. 4 Haute Couture. Fall-Winter 1989-90. Detail of jacket embroidered with decorative motif inspired by Hoffmann. Photo Janos Grapow/Archivio Valentino. 5 Haute Couture. Fall-Winter 1989-90. Crocodile, white lizard, and python skin purse with motifs inspired by Hoffmann. Photo Archivio Valentino. 6 Haute Couture. Spring-Summer 1969. Trouser suit with print inspired by Beardsley. Photo François Leroy-Beaulieu/Archivio Valentino. 7 Haute Couture. Spring-Summer 1969. Dress with geometric appliqué motif. Photo David Bailey/Archivio Valentino. 8 Haute Couture. Spring-Summer 1970. Blouse in op art fabric with "Valentino" written in various sizes. Photo Archivio Valentino. 9 Haute Couture. Spring-Summer 1987. Evening gown with strongly contrasted black-and-white chevron motif. Photo David Bailey/Archivio Valentino. 10 Haute Couture. Fall-Winter 1965-66. White chamois boots with black pom-poms. Photo Archivio Valentino. 11 Haute Couture. Fall-Winter 1967-68. Checked and striped suit with striking black-and-white graphic motifs. Photo Archivio Valentino. 12 Haute Couture. Fall-Winter 1966-67. Dress and overcoat with geometric motifs inspired by Vasarely's paintings. Photo Archivio Valentino. 13 Haute Couture. Spring-Summer 1966. Two black-and-white sequin suits and "box" hats. Photo Henry Clarke/Courtesy *Vogue* © 1966 Condé Nast Publications Inc.

Page 140

1 Haute Couture. Spring-Summer 1987. Ribbons laced through loops in printed silk dresses. Photo Archivio Valentino. 2 Haute Couture. Spring-Summer 1983. Evening gown with large bow at back. Photo Marco Glaviano/Archivio Valentino. 3 Haute Couture. Spring-Summer 1983. Detail of wide-brimmed hat with large bow at the front. Photo Arthur Elgort/Archivio Valentino. 4 Haute Couture. Fall-Winter 1987-88. Red evening dress with asymmetrical hem and large black bow. Photo David Bailey/Archivio Valentino. 5 Prêt-à-porter. Fall-Winter 1987-88. Black velvet dress featuring a white ribbon looped through the sleeve. Photo Archivio Valentino. 6 Haute Couture. Fall-Winter 1967-68. Sergio Valente's hairstyle with bows for Valentino. Photo Archivio Valentino. 7 Haute Couture. Spring-Summer 1989. Evening gown with white collar and black bows. Photo David Bailey/Archivio Valentino. 8 Haute Couture. Fall-Winter 1987-88. Detail of overlapped neckline with looped bow. Photo Gianni Giansanti/Sygma/Grazia Neri. 9 Prêt-à-porter. Fall-Winter 1982-83. Black velvet evening dress with large bow and white quilted peplum. Photo Rico Puhlmann/Archivio Valentino.

Page 146

Accessories. 1 Jewelry. Fall-Winter 1984-85. Large bow cuff bracelet. Photo Oliviero Toscani/Archivio Valentino. 2 Haute Couture. Fall-Winter 1985-86. Eighteenth-century style rhinestone jewelry. Photo Terence Donovan/Archivio Valentino. 3 Prêt-à-porter. Fall-Winter 1985-86. Ornament in the shape of bows of diminishing sizes. Photo Archivio Valentino. 4 Haute Couture. Fall-Winter 1982-83. Black evening dress with asymmetrical neckline and white sash with large bow at the shoulder. Photo Barry McKinley/Archivio Valentino. 5 Prêt-à-porter. Fall-Winter 1985-86. Draped red dress with black bow clasp. Photo Terence Donovan/Archivio Valentino. 6 Prêt-à-porter. Spring-Summer 1984. Detail of bow bracelet. Photo Helmut Newton/Archivio Valentino. 7 Haute Couture. Fall-Winter 1984-85. Detail of white evening dress with bared back, closed by a bow. Photo Arthur Elgort/Courtesy *Vogue* © 1985 Les Publications Condé Nast S.A. 8 Haute Couture. Spring-Summer 1985. Detail of draped red evening gown and black bow clasps. Photo John Swannell/Archivio Valentino. 9 Prêt-à-porter. Spring-Summer 1985. Jeweled bow on back of evening gown. Photo Irving Penn/Courtesy *Vogue* © 1985 Condé Nast Publications Inc. 10 Haute Couture. Spring-Summer 1984. Detail of bow-shaped jewelry. Photo Helmut Newton/Archivio Valentino.

Page 158

1 Haute Couture. Spring-Summer 1969. Little double-polka-dot dress and transparent polka-dot tights. Photo Archivio Valentino. 2 Haute Couture. Spring-Summer 1971. Maxi polka-dot chemisier open in front and cinched by a belt with oriental-style buckle over short shorts with fishnet tights. Photo Bob Krieger. 3 Haute Couture. Spring-Summer 1983. Silk tunic with large polka-dot motif; white cuffs and skirt; broad-brimmed hat with large bow. Photo Avi Meroz. 4 Haute Couture. Spring-Summer 1983. Chinese-style tunics over trousers with small polka-dot motif in negative and positive. Photo Yokosuka/Archivio Valentino. 5 Les Enfants. Fall-Winter 1984-85. Polka-dot dress with

large bow and white collar. Photo Danilo Frontini/Archivio Valentino. **6** Prêt-à-porter. Spring-Summer 1984. Suit with long polka-dot silk jacket, tight skirt, and "sailor" style beret. Photo Helmut Newton/Archivio Valentino. **7** Haute Couture. Spring-Summer 1983. Polka-dot silk evening gown with drapery and knotted bows. Photo Giampaolo Barbieri. **8** Haute Couture. Spring-Summer 1987. Austere "school girl" evening dress with large white collar. Photo Cristina Ghergo/Archivio Valentino. **9** Haute Couture. Spring-Summer 1988. Black suit with black-and-white polka-dot scarf. Photo David Bailey/Archivio Valentino.

Page 200

1 Haute Couture. Fall-Winter 1987-88. Cashmere wool jacquard coat in python-skin motif with sable collar. Photo David Bailey. **2** Prêt-à-porter. Fall-Winter 1988-89. Printed fake fur. **3** Prêt-à-porter. Fall-Winter 1987-88. Rollneck and cardigan twin-set with accessories in leopard motifs. **4** Haute Couture. Fall-Winter 1969-70. Trouser suit: crocodile jacket with sable-trimmed sleeves to match the sable fur hat. **5** Haute Couture. Fall-Winter 1966-67. Leopard-print ensemble with geometric line and high waist. **6** Prêt-à-porter. Fall-Winter 1987-88. Animal print suit with fur trim. **7** Prêt-à-porter. Fall-Winter 1987-88. Leopard spot print for a short fur-trimmed redingote. Photo Steven Meisel. **8** Haute Couture. Fall-Winter 1967-68. Tigers on the palazzo pajama with long-sleeved tunic and tights embroidered in the same motif. Photo Bela Cseh. **9** Prêt-à-porter. Fall-Winter 1988-89. Trouser suit in fake fur with black-and-white pinto spots. Photo Marc Hispard/*Elle*/Grazia Neri. **10** Haute Couture. Fall-Winter 1987-88. Green python-skin jacket with sable cuffs and fur hat.

Page 269

1 Haute Couture. Fall-Winter 1985-86. Evening dress with plunging neckline and an embroidered skirt. Photo Terence Donovan. **2** Haute Couture. Fall-Winter 1986-87. Dress in large floral print fabric and matching wrap. Photo Oliviero Toscani. **3** Haute Couture. Fall-Winter 1982-83. Evening gown featuring a velvet bodice trimmed with red and purple, scalloped taffeta flounces and a long, side-slit, red crepe skirt. Photo Barry McKingley. **4** Haute Couture. Fall-Winter 1986-87. Ball gown with severe line and gold fur hat and belt. Photo Terence Donovan/*L'Officiel*. **5** Haute Couture. Fall-Winter 1990-91. Brown draped dress. Photo David Bailey/Archivio Valentino. **6** Haute Couture. Fall-Winter 1989-90. Polka-dot evening dress. Photo Walter Chin. **7** Haute Couture. Spring-Summer 1988. Crinoline dress with, wide horizontal black, white, and pink bands. Photo David Bailey. **8** Haute Couture. Fall-Winter 1983-84. Black sequined evening dress with "galaxy" motif embroidered over one shoulder and long-fringed sleeves. Photo Barry McKinley. **9** Haute Couture. Fall-Winter 1990-91. Jet-beaded evening dress with bow at the waist. Photo David Bailey

Page 272

1 Haute Couture. Spring-Summer 1987. Black evening dress with short torero-style bolero embroidered with seedbeads. Photo Alex Chatelain. **2** Haute Couture. Fall-Winter 1986-87. Jewellike bodice all in openwork embroidery with sable trim and brown velvet skirt. Photo François Lamy/Courtesy *Harper's Bazaar Italia*. **3** Prêt-à-porter. Fall-Winter 1988-89. Elegant evening gown with Louis XVI-style embroidered bodice, with black and silver sequins, over a midnight blue taffeta and lace skirt. **4** Haute Couture. Fall-Winter 1988-89. Satin evening dress with sable-trimmed jacket, embroidered with baroque-inspired motifs. Photo David Bailey. **5** Haute Couture. Fall-Winter 1988-89. Blue evening dress with draped bodice, corset belt with exquisite embroidery; satin skirt and flowing wrap. Photo David Bailey. **6** Prêt-à-porter. Fall-Winter 1986-87. Black evening dress with cuffs and sash in gold. Photo David Bailey. **7** Haute Couture. Fall-Winter 1989-90. Satin evening gown with embroidery and appliqué flowers on off-the-shoulder fitted sleeves; interlaced ribbons at the neckline accent the bodice. Photo Matthew Rolston. **8** Prêt-à-porter. Fall-Winter 1987-88. Pink satin evening dress with fitted bodice and double peplum. **9** Prêt-à-porter. Spring-Summer 1990. Silk crepe evening gown with exquisite insets of embroidered flowers with silver leaves. Photo Eamonn McCabe/*Marie-Claire* © Mondadori Press.

valentino

Collezione Primavera-Estate 1966

brunetta

Printed in Italy
by Grafiche Bierre s.r.l. (CO)
June 1991